T

Boo

Sarah Stancliffe gained a large and enthusiastic following as the cookery writer on the *Church Times*. She is the author of *The Christian Aid Book of Bread*.

She is married to David Stancliffe, the Bishop of Salisbury, and their hospitality is renowned.

The Christian Aid Book of Simple Feasts

Sarah Stancliffe

First published in 2007 by the Canterbury Press Norwich
(a publishing imprint of Hymns Ancient & Modern Limited,
a registered charity)
13–17 Long Lane, London EC1A 9PN

www.scm-canterburypress.co.uk

British Library Cataloguing in Publication data

A catalogue record for this book is available
from the British Library

ISBN 978-1-85311-836-4

Typeset by Regent Typesetting, London
Printed in the UK by
CPI Bookmarque, Croydon, CRO 4TD

Contents

Acknowledgements

My thanks to Christine Smith of Canterbury Press and Paula Clifford of Christian Aid for encouraging me to write this book, and to Mary Matthews, Editorial Manager, for her quiet efficiency in its production. To Kathryn Wolfendale, copy-editor, and Jane Isaac, proofreader, whose eagle eyes have saved many mistakes.

To all the clergy wives and others who responded to my cry for help, even if I haven't used all their suggestions. Much good cooking goes on in clergy households and at retreat centres.

To the cookery writers whose ideas have informed my cooking over many years: Elizabeth David, Jane Grigson, Claire Macdonald of Macdonald, Delia Smith, Nicola Cox and especially to Josceline Dimbleby, many of whose inspired recipes appear in these pages.

To the publishers, Penguin and Martin Books for permission to print recipes by Jane Grigson, Elizabeth David and Rosamond Richardson.

To all our friends, colleagues and family, who by eating often with us, encourage us to try new recipes as well as old favourites.

Finally, to Emma who so bravely transcribes my scrawl onto disk, for her cheerful patience and broadmindedness (she herself is a vegetarian).

Foreword

Sharing food is a recurring theme in the Bible. The Old and New Testaments are full of shared meals, from the story of Abraham and Sarah who entertained two guests who turned out to be angels, to Jesus' feeding of the five thousand. And the Last Supper of course became a focal point of the Christian faith.

Hospitality – offering a welcome to friend and stranger – is a crucial part of Jesus' ministry. Jesus spent his time on earth feeding people, attending to their material and spiritual needs. He healed them of their physical afflictions and gave them food so they could all feast together. By giving and receiving welcome, Jesus demonstrated God's welcome to all humanity.

The Christian Aid Book of Simple Feasts is a practical book for anyone wanting to extend hospitality, and especially for the largely unsung heroes who cater for larger numbers in their homes and at church celebrations. And it is a reflection of one of Christian Aid's core beliefs – that all should be included in the feast of life.

You'll find traditional recipes, including a sumptuous Easter Lamb and a classic Summer Pudding, as well as international flavours from an Atlas Mountain Soup to a Vegetable Khichdi. Fairtrade ingredients are used wherever possible, and the large number of vegetarian recipes encourages us all to use seasonal produce from local farmers' markets.

Foreword

As the development agency of 41 sponsoring churches in the UK and Ireland, Christian Aid works to empower some of the world's poorest communities, working through over 700 partner organisations in nearly 50 countries. And an important part of this work is responding to emergencies that deprive people, at least temporarily, of the means to feed themselves.

Thank you for buying this book. You are strengthening our support for some of the world's poorest communities and enabling them to share with us the gift of life.

Daleep Mukarji
Director, Christian Aid

Introduction

Gathering for food around a common table is part of our Christian tradition, as indeed of other religions, and a hospitable table is one which expands for unexpected guests and attends to each one's needs.

This book is intended for anyone who finds themselves cooking for more guests than usual and wants to enjoy the party as well as provide for it. Many of the recipes can be made in advance so that last-minute preparation is minimal. There is guidance on how much to cook for large numbers, so that you are not left with pans full of boiled rice and bowls full of dressed salad. Most thoughtful cooks nowadays want to buy ethically; this may mean searching out fairly-traded imported foods with the Fairtrade logo, supporting local food producers where possible, buying free-range eggs and poultry and well-farmed meat and fish. None of this comes cheap, so those of us on a limited budget must buy carefully and perhaps consider serving less meat and more vegetables, even at parties. You will find many delicious vegetarian recipes among my suggestions.

My own experience has been over 40 years in a clergy household, most recently in a large and lovely house in a cathedral close where we entertain many different guests, from the famished vagrant unexpectedly (but quite often) at the door to the ordination candidates on retreat, the regular committees and councils needing working lunches and suppers to the annual gatherings for retired bishops and deans, newly-arrived or soon-to-depart clergy, visitors from our links in France, Sudan and Latvia and so on. These parties may entail sit-down but informal suppers for 25–30, grander three- or four-course dinner parties (silver and candles) for up to 16, or more often, larger buffet parties where fork food is the best answer. Family gatherings grow too as the grandchildren multiply and bring friends and then there are weekends when we muster our musician friends and need to feed bodies as well as souls. I hope the recipes I have chosen reflect all these different needs and styles.

Planning a party

In most houses, even large ones like our present one, the number of guests determines the style of party, so be clear in your mind what you are aiming at. When you send out invitations, be as helpful to the guests as possible – let them know who else is coming so that they may share lifts, and encourage them to tell you of any special diets or allergies they may have. According to the constraints of your house, plan how the party will work geographically; where will guests leave their coats, collect a drink and gather before the food happens? In the summer, might it be possible to spill out into the garden? If you are giving a stand-up or perch-on-a-chair fork buffet, how will access to the food be best managed? Is there a second room where puddings might be laid out? One way to encourage mingling even at sit-down parties is to lay out puddings in a separate room and get your guests to go and choose their own – it also gives them a chance to use the cloakroom, and even to change their neighbour if they like. Not to mention stretching their legs.

Having decided upon the sort of party and the likely guests, then you have the fun of *choosing the menu.* You need to ask yourself some questions:

What will your guests enjoy?	Exotic or traditional? British or foreign? Comfort food or new experience?

One lesson I have learned over the years is to keep the main course simple, especially for larger parties. Do not give people too much choice – one or two main dishes and a vegetarian option are enough. You can make an exotic spicy stew with a more traditional one as an alternative and choose vegetables that will complement either. Do provide plenty of the vegetarian dish, even if you are only expecting one or two vegetarians, because meat-eaters nowadays will be tempted by the appetising veggie option and often come back for it instead of a second helping of meat.

When it comes to puddings, the strategy changes and a choice of three or four is a good idea. People do love puddings and if, like us, you don't have them every day, a choice of spectacular puddings makes the party really special. It also gives you a chance to cater for different needs – a fruit salad for the figure-conscious, something richly chocolate and maybe a cake, a trifle or a tart. For grander parties, some individual custards, wine jellies or chocolate mousses scattered among the puddings are attractive.

You will notice that I have only mentioned main courses and puddings so far. If you are serving a soup or starter you will need to consider your crockery; using bowls for soup may mean you need puddings on plates. Or can the soup be had from a mug? Or can you persuade someone to wash up the soup bowls in time for them to reappear for pudding? Have you the cutlery needed for the various courses or will you need to borrow? Remember that if your largest bowl is full of lemon mousse, you cannot also use it for a green salad. If you are all sitting down, are there enough cruets to go round? Taking care to think out the details in advance makes the actual party day much more straightforward and relaxed.

Finally, cheese or not cheese at the end of the meal? It's up to you; we do not always offer it – these days it is more often served at lunch after a bowl of soup – but having said that, some people do relish cheese, even after a good helping of meat, so I quite often put a small cheeseboard beside the puddings. Then guests can choose whether to eat it before or after the sweet things.

The other consideration in planning the menu is balancing the colours, textures and taste of the food. If you serve a creamy soup, don't choose a main course involving cream and then a creamy mousse. If the first course involves green leaves, don't serve a green salad next or a green jelly for pudding. This may sound obvious but it is easy to consider courses separately and not see the whole.

This is also the time to plan which food can be prepared in advance and which courses should be hot and which cold. Our most usual pattern for winter buffet parties is hot main course and cold puddings, but in summer we might serve a hot potato dish with cold meat or a soup that can be hot or cold. Tarts are usually best served warm rather than hot, and the same is true of some of the Mediterranean-style vegetable dishes (e.g. Stuffed Peppers or Ragoût of Peppers and Onions).

Equipment

Your kitchen equipment needs a little thought, too, especially if you are cooking for crowds more often than just occasionally. Large gratin dishes and mixing bowls can sometimes be picked up second-hand; good-quality large saucepans and casseroles may be harder to come by among the junk bargains but can be found at a reasonable price in the cheaper stores. I bought heavy-based stainless steel pans in Woolworths for the Aga when we moved here and they are doing well 13 years on. I also found medium-sized white dinner plates for £1 each – 20 of those are in constant use. Collect large serving spoons and ladles wherever you go.

Large plastic and light stainless steel bowls are invaluable for holding bulky salads, and large chopping boards are very useful too. Sharp knives, of course. I am not much into machines but would not be without my Kenwood mixer and a small hand-held electric whisk. A tall electric hand-held blender is useful for whizzing soups and sauces in the pan. I can see that a food processor would be good for chopping and slicing and grating but haven't yet got one.

Well-marked measuring jugs are particularly useful when making lots of soup or stew – choose ones with imperial and metric measures. One small gadget I discovered late in life is my zester which is also the best implement for descaling fish. Dishwashers come into their own for large numbers.

Parish meals

Most parishes find themselves gathering for meals several times a year, whether it be when a new vicar arrives, for a Harvest supper, a Lent lunch maybe or a Christmas dinner for older residents. Parish halls and kitchens vary enormously in how well they are equipped; when you are planning such a meal, you need to ask the same questions as for a feast at home:

What sort of meal are we aiming at? Standing or sitting? Hot or cold or a mixture? How will the food be accessible (buffet-style or hand-around or table service?). Do we have the crockery and cutlery we need? Will there be special diets to cater for?

Good delegation is half the battle; gather two or three others (not too many) and agree what you will offer. Play to people's strengths, so that if you know one volunteer makes delicious egg sandwiches but is no good at scones and another is a dab hand at pastry but mean with sandwich fillings, delegate accordingly. Diplomacy may be needed!

A few thoughts about menus for special meals:

Parish bunfights – Aim for simple, satisfying finger food. Well-filled sandwiches are more appetising than bought-in sausage rolls or thin cold quiches. You will need more savouries than sweets, probably, but some small squares of rich chocolate or fruit cake or small éclairs make a fine end to such a party.

Harvest suppers – Make sure the menu reflects the point of the meal; look at the Autumn chapter for seasonal soups or starters. Keep the main course simple; give the same recipe to two or three cooks so each can make it at home and bring it along. The Lentil Moussaka or the Spicy Autumn Vegetable Casserole might be a good veggie option. Remember to reheat casseroles thoroughly and choose vegetables which reheat well – red cabbage, carrot and swede mash, potatoes à la boulangère – see the Seasonal Vegetables chapter.

Lent lunches – Soups are all-important and you will find plenty of recipes in the Winter and Spring sections. Try the two vegetarian pâtés – Potted Lentils with Mushroom and Hummus – with good fresh bread. Soup in mugs is very convenient and cuts down on the washing up. Collect money for a third world cause.

Christmas dinners – Basic cookery books tell you how to cook a turkey; if possible buy a good free-range one rather than a bland mass-produced bird, and try to avoid turkey rolls. Carving needs planning but is much best done shortly before the meal, keeping the meat in a large dish covered with foil in a warm place while you make the gravy and deal with the vegetables.

Consider serving roast pork instead (see recipe, page 24). Vegetarians might enjoy the Christmas Nut Wellington (see recipe, page 73).

Never refuse help with the washing up or moving the furniture!

How to use the recipes

These recipes are designed for cooking in a normal kitchen, not a catering establishment. I have given two sizes for most main course recipes – to feed 6–8 or 20. I hope these are useful bases from which to work out your quantities. Do bear in mind the strange fact that *the more guests you have the less per head they eat*. Not all ingredients need to be multiplied by the same amount when you upsize a recipe, so do read them carefully.

For puddings I have given recipes for 8–10 or 10–12, to fit normal tins and bowls and also because you will be serving several different ones.

For unusually large parties of over 40 people, it is generally wise to enlist a friend or two to share the cooking so that no one is over-burdened. Find out what your friends make well and ask for that when possible. I have tried to indicate in each recipe which stages can be completed in advance.

It is worth getting to know the capacity of your pots and pans; my largest Le Creuset casserole holds 10 pints/5.6 litres and will fit enough stew for 20 people. My deep preserving pan holds 20 pints/11.2 litres so is useful for cooking lots of rice or a whole ham. I have two steamers which sit above ordinary saucepans and I know that each holds enough new potatoes to feed 10–12 people.

1 The ingredients are listed in order of use.
2 Quantities are given in imperial and metric measures – use one or the other but not a mixture.
3 Teaspoons is abbreviated **tsp** and tablespoons as **Tbsp**. Use level spoonfuls unless otherwise instructed.
4 Eggs are medium-sized unless otherwise specified.
5 Oven temperatures are given in Gas Mark, Fahrenheit (F) and Centigrade (C).
6 **!** indicates preparation needed sometime before, e.g. overnight soaking.

7 ☺ indicates an exceptionally easy, quick recipe: 5–30 minutes preparation; cooking may be longer.
8 V indicates a vegetarian recipe.

Safety

When you are feeding many people, you do need to be extra scrupulous over food hygiene and safety. We invested in a larder fridge some years ago and it is a huge help in storing food which needs to be kept cool. The most important rules are:

- Make sure frozen food is thawed slowly and cooked or reheated thoroughly, especially meat.
- Refrigerate food to be kept as soon as it is cool.
- Dried beans need to be boiled hard for 10 minutes to destroy toxins before simmering till tender.
- Cooked rice needs thorough reheating if it is to be reused in a hot dish.
- Warn pregnant and elderly guests if your food includes raw eggs.

Fairtrade and ethical shopping

Food awarded the Fairtrade label has to meet agreed international Fairtrade standards. The producers receive a minimum price to cover the cost of sustainable production and an extra premium to invest in social or economic development projects.

Anybody concerned about the development of the third world and justice in economic activity must support the Fairtrade movement. As consumers, we have successfully persuaded even large retailers that there is a demand for Fairtrade products, and more and more of these are becoming available.

Among British supermarkets, the Co-operative Society stands out for its commitment to a wide range of fairly traded goods, and others are extending their range. Not only coffee, cocoa and chocolate and bananas come Fairtrade nowadays, but sugar, dried fruit, nuts, biscuits, cake, fruit juices and wines, honey, rice and pasta and a host of sweet snacks and savouries. Oxfam shops sell a wide range.

To keep up to date with what is available and where, log on to www.fairtrade.org.uk

Two useful addresses:

Traidcraft plc
Kingsway
Gateshead
Tyne and Wear
NE11 0NE
Telephone: 0191 491 0591

Cafédirect plc
New City Cloisters
Suite B2
19 Old Street
London
EC1V 9FR
Telephone: 020 7490 9520

These organisations give advice on how to buy catering packs of Fairtrade food. Traidcraft have special accounts for caterers.

Apart from buying all we can fairly traded, how can we shop ethically? In many parts of England, supermarkets have pretty much the monopoly of food retailing; here in Salisbury, for instance, we no longer have a greengrocer in town, though twice a week we do have a market. The obvious advice is to buy local produce as much as you can, support your farmers' markets, ask your butcher where he gets his meat and when you buy fish, find out where it is from. None of us can lead an ethically pure life but we can show that we care where our food comes from and how it is produced. For me this means buying free-range meat as far as possible; to balance the budget, choose recipes using less meat and more vegetables. Even at a dinner party, if you serve a good rich soup first, you don't need to serve huge portions of meat next, so long as there are delicious vegetables to fill the plate and, of course, puddings to follow.

Seasonal Recipes

Autumn

September, October, November

'Season of mists and mellow fruitfulness . . .' and season of plenty in our temperate Western climate – until now, anyway. Time for Harvest suppers to celebrate the result of all the farmers' labour, for the plumpest peppers, for wild mushrooms, Halloween pumpkins, runner beans and autumn raspberries. Make the most of any gluts – apples, courgettes or green tomatoes – and lay down chutneys for the leaner winter months.

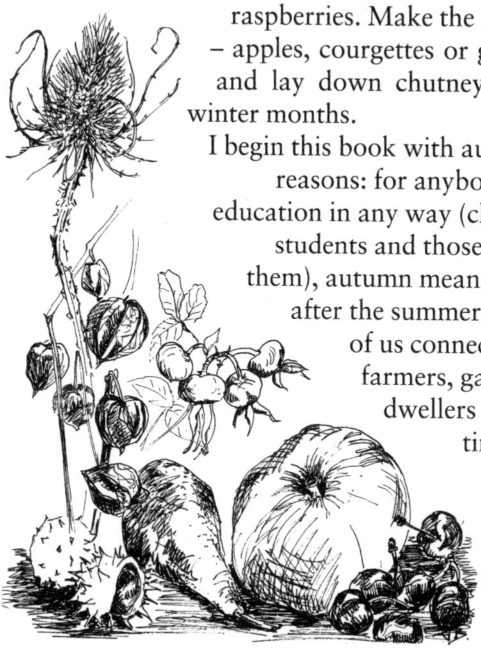

I begin this book with autumn for several reasons: for anybody involved with education in any way (children, teachers, students and those who provide for them), autumn means new beginnings after the summer break. For those of us connected to the land – farmers, gardeners, country dwellers and cooks, it is a time of abundance and plenty, so a good time to focus on the kitchen.

Autumn

Soups and Starters

Pumpkin Soup
Golden West Country Soup
Split Pea Soup
Jerusalem Artichoke Soup
Smoked Mackerel Pâté
Lentil Salad with Eggs and Olives
Onion, Anchovy and Olive Tart

Main Courses

Spicy Lamb with Mint and Spinach
Manzo Stufato (Beef and Pepper Stew)
Chicken, Rice and Prunes with Curry Sauce
Roast Pork with Apple and Walnut Stuffing
V Lentil Moussaka
V Spicy Autumn Vegetable Casserole
V Mushroom Cheesy Bake
Mum's Fish Pie
V Ratatouille with Eggs

Puddings

Apple Curd Tart
Tropical Fruit Compôte
Apricot or Prune Mousse
Springfield Pear Cake
Collette's Chocolate Roulade
Mrs Goronwy's Marmalade Tart
Veiled Farmer's Daughter
Raspberry and Ginger Shortbread

Soups and Starters

PUMPKIN SOUP

Pumpkins and squashes of all kinds are available in supermarkets and garden shops these days – use them to make this lovely spicy golden soup.

For 6–8	*For 20*
4oz/125g butter	8oz/250g butter
2 onions, peeled and chopped	4 onions, peeled and chopped
2lb/1kg pumpkin, deseeded, peeled and cubed	5lb/2.5kg pumpkin, deseeded, peeled and cubed
½ tsp grated nutmeg	1 tsp grated nutmeg
½ tsp ground ginger	1 tsp ground ginger
1 pint/600ml vegetable stock	3 pints/1.8 litres vegetable stock
1 pint/600ml milk	2 pints/1.2 litres milk
salt and pepper	salt and pepper
¼ pint/150ml single cream	½ pint/300ml single cream
croûtons (optional)	croûtons (optional)

Melt the butter in a large saucepan, soften the chopped onion for a few minutes in the butter, then add the cubed pumpkin flesh and turn over and over to coat each cube. Add the grated nutmeg and ground ginger and cook for a minute or two. Then add the vegetable stock, bring gently to the boil, cover and simmer until soft and pulpy – about 15 minutes.

Liquidise with the milk, in batches if need be, return to the pan to heat through, taste and season with salt and pepper.

Stir in the cream just before serving and serve the croûtons (see page 202) alongside.

GOLDEN WEST COUNTRY SOUP

Another golden autumn soup, this one from the West Country, hence the cider. It is a good example of the classic method of making soup: gently sweat your vegetables in butter before adding the liquid. My thanks to Liz Bourke for this one.

For 6–8	*For 20*
4oz/125g butter	6oz/200g butter
1lb/450g carrots, diced	2½lb/1kg carrots, diced
1lb/450g potatoes, diced	2½lb/1kg potatoes, diced
2 cloves garlic	4 cloves garlic
2 × 14oz/400g tins tomatoes	4 × 14oz/400g tins tomatoes
1½ pints/800ml medium or sweet cider	3½ pints/2 litres medium or sweet cider
1½ pints/800ml vegetable stock	3½ pints/2 litres vegetable stock
salt and pepper	salt and pepper
chopped parsley or coriander	chopped parsley or coriander

Melt the butter in a large saucepan and gently sweat the carrots and potatoes until softening – about 5 minutes. Do not let them brown.

Crush the garlic cloves and add them to the pan with the tomatoes, cider and vegetable stock. Bring to the boil, cover and simmer until the vegetables are soft. Season with salt and pepper.

Liquidise in batches and blend until smooth. Return to the pan, reheat, taste and adjust seasoning.

Garnish with chopped parsley or coriander and serve in warm bowls.

SPLIT PEA SOUP

Dried pulses such as lentils or split peas make wonderful warming soups; this is a thick, semi-liquidised soup which needs a bowl and spoon. With croûtons and grated cheese added, it makes a meal in itself. The idea of liquidising only half the soup is an Italian one but works well with this very English soup. Unless your peas are *very* old, they don't need to be soaked in advance.

For 6–8	*For 20*
3½ pints/2 litres ham or vegetable stock	8 pints/5 litres ham or vegetable stock
12oz/350g split peas	2¼ lb/1kg split peas
2oz/50g butter	5oz/150g butter
1 medium onion, chopped small	3 onions, chopped small
1 large leek, chopped small	3 leeks, chopped small
2 celery stalks, chopped small	5 celery stalks, chopped small
1lb/450g potatoes, peeled and chopped small	3lb/1.5kg potatoes, peeled and chopped small
salt and pepper	salt and pepper
croûtons (optional)	croûtons (optional)
3oz/100g grated cheese (optional)	8oz/225g grated cheese (optional)

Heat the stock in a large pan, add the split peas and bring to the boil. Cover and simmer gently for 30–40 minutes.

Meanwhile melt the butter in a smaller pan and add the prepared vegetables. Turn them in the butter, cover and sweat for 10–15 minutes, stirring or shaking from time to time.

Add the softened vegetables to the stock and peas, season lightly with salt and pepper, taking into account the saltiness of your stock, cover and simmer for 30–40 minutes, until the vegetables and peas are really soft.

Liquidise about half of the soup and return to the pan. Taste and adjust the seasoning.

If you are adding cheese, stir it in before adding the croûtons (see page 202) and serving.

JERUSALEM ARTICHOKE SOUP

If you have Jerusalem artichokes in your garden, you will have plenty for this soup, which has a fine flavour in spite of its rather dull colour. If you are buying the artichokes, choose the smoothest ones with fewest knobbles.

For 6–8	*For 20*
4oz/125g butter	6oz/200g butter
2 large onions, peeled and chopped	5 onions, peeled and chopped
1 clove garlic, chopped	2 cloves garlic, chopped
2lb/1kg Jerusalem artichokes	5lb/2.5kg Jerusalem artichokes
1 Tbsp plain flour	2½ Tbsp plain flour
2 pints/1.2 litres chicken or vegetable stock	5 pints/3 litres chicken or vegetable stock
¾ pint/500ml milk	2 pints/1.2 litres milk
salt and pepper	salt and pepper
3 Tbsp single cream	6–8 Tbsp single cream

Scrub and roughly peel the artichokes – don't worry if some skin remains on the knobbly bits but make sure all grit and earth is removed.

Cut them into small pieces. Melt the butter in a large saucepan and add the onions, artichokes and garlic. Stir to turn them all in the butter, then cover and stew gently for 5–10 minutes, shaking the pan from time to time. Add the flour and stir well.

Pour in the stock gradually, cover and simmer until the vegetables are cooked – about 20 minutes.

Liquidise in batches, return to the pan, taste and season. Stir in the cream just before serving.

SMOKED MACKEREL PÂTÉ ☺

Fish pâtés are very easy to make and smoked mackerel makes a robust pâté for the autumn. You can make it up to a week in advance; simply cover the bowl with cling film and refrigerate. If you choose peppered mackerel, omit the pepper in the recipe.

For 6–8	*For 20–25*
1lb/450g smoked mackerel fillets	3lb/1.35kg smoked mackerel fillets
5fl oz/150ml sour cream or crème fraîche	15fl oz/450ml sour cream or crème fraîche
4oz/120g low fat soft cheese	12oz/350g low fat soft cheese
4 tsp creamed horseradish	3 Tbsp creamed horseradish
juice of half a lemon	juice of 1½ lemons
salt and black pepper	salt and black pepper

Remove any skin from the mackerel. Flake it into the liquidiser or food processor, add all the other ingredients and whiz until smooth. Taste and adjust seasoning. Pack into a pretty bowl, cover with clingfilm and chill.

Serve with crusty bread or wholemeal toast.

Note: If you have no liquidiser or food processor, you can mash the ingredients with a fork to make a coarser pâté.

LENTIL SALAD WITH EGGS AND OLIVES

Lentils are widely available and come in three main kinds. Red split lentils cook very quickly to a mush and are useful in soups. Brown lentils and slate-grey Le Puy lentils (both of these are sometimes called 'continental lentils') keep their shape and texture when cooked and are useful both as a vegetable and as a substitute for minced meat in vegetarian dishes.

Here is a lentil salad which makes a good autumn starter.

For 6–8	*For 20*
1lb/450g continental lentils	2¼lb/1kg continental lentils
1 large onion, peeled	2 large onions, peeled
1 bay leaf	2–3 bay leaves
water to cover	water to cover
6 Tbsp olive oil	½ pint/280ml olive oil
2 Tbsp wine vinegar	6 Tbsp wine vinegar
salt and pepper	salt and pepper
2 Tbsp chopped fresh herbs (e.g. parsley, chives, coriander)	5–6 Tbsp chopped fresh herbs (e.g. parsley, chives, coriander)
2 hard-boiled eggs, shelled	4 hard-boiled eggs, shelled
12 small black olives	20 small black olives
½ tin anchovy fillets	1 tin anchovy fillets
2 large red peppers, grilled and skinned	4 large red peppers, grilled and skinned

First pour the lentils onto a flat dish and pick out any obvious pieces of grit. Then put them in a large pan with the onion and bay leaf and cover generously with cold water. Bring to the boil, cover the pan and simmer gently for 30–40 minutes until tender, adding more hot water as required to keep them from boiling dry.

While they are cooking, you can hard-boil the eggs, mix the oil and the vinegar in a large bowl to make a vinaigrette, and grill the peppers (don't be tempted to use raw peppers – the smoky sweet taste of grilled ones is important to the dish).

When the lentils are done, drain them in a sieve, remove the onion and bay leaf and tip the lentils straight into the bowl with the vinaigrette. Turn them in the dressing and season with salt and pepper and leave to cool.

All this can be done a day or even two in advance. Keep them covered in a cool larder or fridge.

To finish the dish, stir in the chopped fresh herbs (spring onion can replace chives and you can vary the other herbs) and turn it all into a serving dish. Then add the hard-boiled eggs, either chopped and stirred in or sliced and laid on top, the olives (ones with stones have much better flavour but do warn your guests), the anchovies torn into pieces, and the red pepper cut into strips.

Serve with fresh bread as a delicious and economical starter.

ONION, ANCHOVY AND OLIVE TART

A pastry starter can be versatile because your guests can either eat it in the hand with their pre-supper drinks, or sitting down with knife and fork. This tart is a version of the classic 'pissaladière' from southern France, made with pastry instead of bread dough. It does take a lot of onions but can be made well in advance. Using shallow Swiss-roll tins (1 for the smaller amount, 3 for the larger) you can easily control the number of portions by judicious division when you cut it up. Bought pastry is fine in this recipe.

For 6–8	*For 20*
3lb/1.4kg onions, thinly sliced	9lb/4kg onions, thinly sliced
4 Tbsp olive oil	12 Tbsp olive oil
2 cloves garlic, crushed	4 cloves garlic, crushed
salt and pepper	salt and pepper
1lb/450g shortcrust pastry	3lb/1.4kg shortcrust pastry
2oz/50g tin of anchovies in oil	3 × 2oz/50g tins of anchovies in oil
12 black olives, pitted	30 black olives, pitted
dried thyme or oregano	dried thyme or oregano

Heat the oil in a large heavy saucepan, stir in the onions and garlic and cook, uncovered, over gentle heat for at least 30 minutes (larger quantities will take longer), stirring occasionally until the onions are melting into a soft mass and just beginning to caramelise. This slow cooking is essential to the final flavour of the tart, bringing out all the sweetness of the onion.

While the onions are cooking, brush a shallow Swiss-roll tin (10½ × 15½in/26 × 40cm) with olive oil, roll out your pastry and cover the base and sides of the tin.

When the onions are ready, remove from the heat and

season with salt and pepper. Spread them all over the pastry base and into the corners. Using a small knife blade, lift the anchovy fillets one by one out of their tins (keep the oil), tear them in half lengthwise and lay them diagonally over the onion base, making a sort of lattice pattern. Then break each olive into 2 or 3 pieces and lay them, shiny side up, among the anchovies.

(At this stage you can keep the tart, uncooked, in a cool larder or fridge for a day or two, continuing the recipe an hour or so before your guests arrive. Or you could complete the recipe earlier in the day, baking and all, let it cool and then reheat it in a warm oven before serving.)

Preheat the oven to Gas 7/425F/220C. Sprinkle the thyme or oregano over the tart, drizzle the oil left in the anchovy tin over the whole thing and bake in a hot oven for 20–25 minutes until the pastry is golden.

Serve warm, cut into suitable slices (smaller if for eating in the hand, larger if sitting down).

Main Courses

SPICY LAMB WITH MINT AND SPINACH

This is a good dish to serve as part of a hot buffet, alongside a blander option. Rice or nan breads go well with it. Thanks to Helen Lambie for this one.

For 6–8	*For 20*
2½lb/1kg diced lamb (shoulder)	6½lb/3kg diced lamb (shoulder)
3 fresh chillies, chopped	6 fresh chillies, chopped
3 cloves garlic, chopped	6 cloves garlic, chopped
spices, 2 tsp each of turmeric, cumin seeds and cardamom seeds, crushed	spices, 4 tsp each of turmeric, cumin seeds and cardamom seeds, crushed
2 Tbsp mint, chopped	6 Tbsp mint, chopped
1lb/450g frozen spinach (thawed but not drained)	2½lb/1kg frozen spinach (thawed but not drained)
¾ pint/400ml single cream or full cream yogurt	2 pints/1 litre single cream or full cream yogurt
salt and pepper	salt and pepper
1oz/25g toasted flaked almonds for garnish	2oz/50g toasted flaked almonds for garnish
extra cream or yogurt to garnish	extra cream or yogurt to garnish

In a capacious casserole, dry fry the lamb with the chillies, garlic and spices until sealed – with the larger quantities you'll need to do this in batches. Add the mint and spinach with its thawed water and simmer for 30–40 minutes until the lamb is tender. Stir in the cream or yogurt and heat through for 5 more minutes. Taste and season, adding a little water or stock if it is too thick. Serve with some more cream or yogurt poured over and sprinkled with toasted flaked almonds.

Vegetarians could adapt this recipe by substituting chickpeas for the lamb: allow 6oz/160g dry chickpeas for every 1lb/450g meat. Soak them overnight and cook before using.

MANZO STUFATO (BEEF AND PEPPER STEW)

! 3 hours or more to marinate the meat

This beef and pepper stew was first created by David in our early holidays in Tuscany and he always makes it. Use shin, which is tougher and cheaper than most beef and makes a wonderful succulent stew with long slow cooking.

For 6–8	*For 20*
3lb/1.4kg shin of beef, thickly cut	9lb/4.2kg shin of beef, thickly cut
Marinade	*Marinade*
a large tumbler of robust red wine	enough red wine to cover the meat
1 large onion, chopped	3 large onions, chopped
3–4 cloves garlic, crushed	6–8 cloves garlic, crushed
thyme, freshly ground pepper	thyme, freshly ground pepper
3 Tbsp olive oil	6–8 Tbsp olive oil
2 large onions, sliced	6 large onions, sliced
3 plump peppers (mixed colours), deseeded and sliced	8–9 plump peppers (mixed colours), deseeded and sliced
2–3 cloves garlic, peeled	4–5 cloves garlic, peeled
thyme and 2 bay leaves	thyme and 4 or 5 bay leaves
another tumbler of red wine	2 or 3 tumblers of red wine
a dozen black olives	2 dozen black olives
salt and pepper	salt and pepper

First, the marinading: lay the beef in a dish or bowl and cover with the marinade ingredients. Leave for 3 hours or longer in a cool place.

Lift the pieces of meat out of the marinade and dry them on kitchen paper. Heat the olive oil in a large, heavy fireproof casserole and brown the meat, in batches if need be. When all are browned, arrange layers of meat with onions and peppers between each layer. Add the marinade together with the fresh garlic, herbs and the second tumbler of wine. Let it all bubble fiercely for 5 minutes or so.

Reduce the heat, cover the pan and simmer over a low heat for 2½–3 hours, till the meat is really tender.

Fifteen minutes before serving, add a handful of black olives, taste and adjust seasoning.

Serve with rice, pasta or mashed potato.

CHICKEN, RICE AND PRUNES WITH CURRY SAUCE

Chicken goes a long way when taken off the bone and mixed in with rice. This recipe came from my grandmother and is always popular. The mild curry sauce and the mango chutney remind us of how gladly we adapted Indian cooking to our nineteenth-century tastes.

For 6–8	*For 20*
1 large free-range chicken	2 large free-range chickens
8oz/225g prunes	1¼lb/550g prunes
2 leeks, trimmed and halved	4 leeks, trimmed and halved
water, salt and peppercorns	water, salt and peppercorns
1lb/450g long grain rice	2lb/1kg long grain rice
For the sauce	*For the sauce*
2oz/50g butter	6oz/150g butter
1 heaped Tbsp flour	3 heaped Tbsp flour
1–2 tsp curry powder or paste	3–5 tsp curry powder or paste
1 pint/570ml of the chicken stock	2½ pints/1.5 litres of the chicken stock
a little milk	¼ pint/150ml milk
salt and pepper	salt and pepper
mango chutney to serve	mango chutney to serve

Put the chicken to boil in a large pan with the prunes and leeks and plenty of salted water. Add the whole peppercorns, bring to the boil, cover and cook gently until the chicken is tender – about an hour.

Take the chicken out of the pan and when it is cool enough to handle, take off all the meat and put it into an ovenproof dish. Fish out the prunes and put them with the chicken, then take out the leeks which can be discarded. Keep the stock on hand for the sauce.

Now melt the butter in a smallish saucepan or a double boiler if you have one, add the flour and curry powder or paste and stir to absorb the butter. Add about a pint of the warm stock gradually as though making a white sauce.

Stir until smooth and let it thicken as it cooks – you are aiming at the consistency of single cream. Add a little milk, taste and adjust the seasoning. In a double boiler, the sauce will stay hot for as long as you like. Otherwise, try not to make it too far in advance. Cover and keep warm.

Reheat the chicken and prunes in a low oven with a few ladlefuls of the stock to moisten them, covered with foil, for about half an hour.

Meanwhile, to cook the rice, bring a really large pan of water to the boil (a 12 pint/7 litre pan for 1lb/450g rice) and salt it. Scatter the rice into it, keeping it at a fast boil for 10–12 minutes, then test a grain. Drain in a large colander as soon as it is cooked and rinse through with hot water, shake the water out and put the rice in a large serving dish. Put the dish in a low oven for a few minutes, turning with a fork. Cover with a clean tea cloth if not serving at once.

To assemble the dish, turn the rice into a hot, capacious serving dish and mix in the chicken pieces and prunes, with some of the stock, which will be absorbed by the rice.

Serve on hot plates with a little curry sauce on each helping and mango chutney alongside. The Chicory, Orange and Fennel Salad (see page 185) would go well with this, or the Green Pea Salad with Ginger and Olives (see page 198).

ROAST PORK WITH APPLE AND WALNUT STUFFING

Weekend groups of musicians need substantial meals to keep them going – a hot Sunday lunch sustains them through the afternoon rehearsal and evening performance. This way of stuffing a large hand of pork has delighted our musician friends for many years. It comes from an early (1979) Sainsbury cookbook by Josceline Dimbleby. These days, hand of pork is not always available, so give your butcher a few days' warning and get him/her to bone it out for you without tying it up afterwards – you will be stuffing it before tying it yourself.

For 10–12

3–4lb/1.3–1.8kg boned hand of pork
1 large apple
a squeeze of lemon
1 Tbsp Fairtrade demerara sugar
2oz/50g fresh brown breadcrumbs
2oz/50g Fairtrade walnuts, chopped
1 egg, beaten
salt and black pepper
2 cloves garlic, crushed
a little olive oil
sea salt
½ pint/300ml beer or cider
1 tsp arrowroot or cornflour

Lay the piece of meat out flat. Peel and grate the apple and put it in a bowl with a squeeze of lemon to stop it going brown. Stir in the sugar, breadcrumbs, walnuts, beaten egg and seasoning. Spread the garlic over the meat and then spoon the stuffing onto it and into any pockets or flaps.

Roll the meat up around the stuffing and fasten with string or skewers. Hands of pork are never an elegant shape so don't worry if it looks ragged. Smear the joint with olive oil, score the skin well with a very sharp knife (if the butcher hasn't) and rub with coarse sea salt to make crisp crackling.

Heat the oven to Gas 8/450F/230C. Put the joint in a roasting pan towards the top of the oven for 20 minutes, then move it to the centre and turn the heat down to Gas 4/350F/180C for another 2–2½ hours, basting occasionally. Plenty of time to get to church and back.

Half an hour before time is up, tip out the fat from the roasting pan and pour the beer or cider in around the pork. This will make a delicious gravy which you can thicken with the arrowroot or cornflour, dissolved in a little water and bubbled up with the juices when you have removed the joint.

Note: If you want to prepare in advance, get the stuffing ready the night before and garlic the meat, but don't stuff it till the morning – if you do, the apple acids will make the whole thing ooze and weep overnight.

LENTIL MOUSSAKA

Lentils can often replace minced meat to good effect and this moussaka recipe is one example. Blanching the aubergine slices instead of frying them saves both time and oil (and waistlines).

For 6–8

2lb/900g aubergines (3–4 large ones)
4 Tbsp olive oil
8oz/225g onion, finely chopped
1 large carrot, finely chopped
2 cloves garlic, finely chopped
2 Tbsp parsley, chopped
10oz/275g continental lentils, picked over
pinch of cayenne pepper
pinch of ground cinnamon
1½–2 pints (850ml–1.2 litres) vegetable stock or water
salt and pepper

For the sauce

2oz/50g butter
1oz/25g flour
¾ pint/425ml milk
salt
1–2oz/25–50g Parmesan to grate

For 20

5lb/2.2kg aubergines (8–10 large ones)
8 Tbsp olive oil
1¼lb/570g onion, finely chopped
3 large carrots, finely chopped
5 cloves garlic, finely chopped
5 Tbsp parsley, chopped
1½lb/700g continental lentils, picked over
1 tsp cayenne pepper
pinch of ground cinnamon
4½–5½ pints (2.7–3.2 litres) vegetable stock or water
salt and pepper

For the sauce

4oz/100g butter
3oz/80g flour
2½ pints/1.5 litres milk
salt
3–4oz/80–120g Parmesan to grate

Bring a large saucepan of water to the boil (probably two if you are making the larger quantity), salt it well and add the aubergines cut across in slices about ¼in/5mm thick. (No need to salt the aubergine in advance.) Bring the pan back to the boil and leave for 3 minutes, uncovered, to soften the aubergine slices. Drain them in a large colander. Set aside.

Heat the oil in another pan, add the onion, carrot, garlic and parsley and stir about over a moderate heat for 5 minutes or so. Add the lentils (picked over for pieces of grit), season with the spices and add enough stock or water to cover generously. Bring to the boil and simmer, covered, until the lentils are cooked – about 30–35 minutes. Stir occasionally and if the lentils absorb the liquid too quickly, add some more. Liquidise half the cooked lentil mixture, then return it to the pan to combine it with the rest. Taste and adjust seasoning. Set aside while you make the sauce.

Melt the butter in a small pan, stir in the flour and cook for a minute or two, then slacken it gradually with the milk, stirring all the time. Season with a little salt, stir in half the grated Parmesan, and simmer to thicken – about 10 minutes. Keep warm on one side while you assemble the moussaka.

Preheat the oven to Gas 5/375F/190C. Oil a baking dish deep enough to take several layers of aubergines and sauce (probably 2 or 3 dishes for the larger quantity). Cover the bottom with a layer of aubergine, then spread half the lentils on top; repeat the layers, finishing with a third layer of aubergine. Pour the sauce over the whole dish, scatter the rest of the Parmesan on top and bake for about 30 minutes, until golden and bubbling.

Serve with crusty bread and a salad.

Note: You can omit the cheese altogether; the sauce will still brown nicely. You can cook the whole thing for longer at a lower temperature and it will keep warm for as long as you need it to – a good-tempered dish.

The lentil mixture makes a good alternative for vegetarians to chilli con carne. For 6–8 make as above, omitting the aubergine and adding 8oz/225g chopped mushrooms and a 14oz/400g tin of red kidney beans, drained, to the vegetables. Spice it well with a fresh chopped chilli or cayenne pepper.

SPICY AUTUMN VEGETABLE CASSEROLE

This spicy stew uses splendidly seasonal vegetables including pumpkin or squash. It has a nice, clean taste and can be made in advance and reheated, though in that case do not add the cabbage till later. The original recipe has been adapted by Gail Ballinger.

For 6–8	*For 20*
2 tsp cumin seeds	3 tsp cumin seeds
3 tsp coriander seeds	5 tsp coriander seeds
1 Tbsp sesame seeds	2 Tbsp sesame seeds
3 Tbsp vegetable oil	5 Tbsp vegetable oil
2 small onions, chopped	3 large onions, chopped
2 cloves garlic, chopped	3 cloves garlic, chopped
1–2 fresh red chillies, chopped	2 fresh red chillies, chopped
12oz/350g pumpkin or squash, deseeded, peeled and cubed	1½lb/700g pumpkin or squash, deseeded, peeled and cubed
8oz/225g celeriac, cubed	1lb/450g celeriac, cubed
8oz/225g swede or parsnip, cubed	1lb/450g swede or parsnip, cubed
1lb/450g large carrots, sliced	2lb/900g large carrots, sliced
1lb/450g tin chickpeas, drained and rinsed	2lb/900g tin chickpeas, drained and rinsed
2 × 14oz/400g tins chopped tomatoes	3–4 × 14oz/400g tins chopped tomatoes
3 tsp oregano or thyme (dried)	5 tsp oregano or thyme (dried)
1½ pints/850ml vegetable stock	2½–3 pints/1–1.5 litres vegetable stock
salt and pepper	salt and pepper
8oz/225g Savoy cabbage, shredded	12oz/350g Savoy cabbage, shredded

Crush the seeds with a pestle and mortar. Fry the onion in the oil in a large casserole until transparent, then add the garlic, seeds and chilli. Stir briefly, then add the pumpkin and root vegetables with a little stock and cook for 4–5 minutes, letting them absorb the oil. Add the chickpeas, tomatoes, oregano or thyme and the remaining stock, season and simmer until it is all cooked – 30 minutes or so. Stir in the cabbage and cook for 3–4 minutes before serving. Does not freeze well.

Can be served on its own, with crusty bread or with mashed potato or rice.

MUSHROOM CHEESY BAKE

This tasty dish of mushrooms and tomatoes baked in a breadcrumb and cheese crust is equally popular with vegetarians and meat-eaters. Because of the quantity of breadcrumbs needed you may not want to attempt the larger size pie, but do try the smaller one.

For 6–8	*For 20*
For the crust	*For the crust*
12oz/350g breadcrumbs, a mixture of brown and white, stale and fresh	2½lb/1.2kg breadcrumbs, a mixture of brown and white, stale and fresh
3 medium onions, grated or finely chopped	9 onions, grated or finely chopped
9oz/250g grated mature cheese	1¾lb/800g grated mature cheese
grated rind of 2 small lemons	grated rind of 6 lemons
juice of 1 lemon	juice of 3 lemons
6oz/175g soft margarine	1lb/500g soft margarine

Mix all the ingredients until tacky. Line a large greased pie dish (use 3, or one enormous baking dish for the larger quantity) with two-thirds of the mixture, pressing it down well over the base and up the sides. Preheat the oven to Gas 5/375F/190C.

For the filling	*For the filling*
8 large tomatoes, chopped	20 large tomatoes, chopped
1lb/450g mushrooms, sliced	3lb/1.4kg mushrooms, sliced
salt and pepper	salt and pepper
juice of 1 lemon	juice of 3 lemons

Fill the pie with these ingredients, then top with the remaining crumb mixture. Press down firmly and dot the top with margarine. Bake for 40–45 minutes (1 hour for the larger amount) in the oven.

Serve hot with a green vegetable or salad.

MUM'S FISH PIE

My mother's observation that most fish pies had too much potato topping and not enough filling led her to invent a pie with fried breadcrumbs on top, in crunchy contrast to the fish, eggs and mushrooms in a smooth sauce below. I add crushed garlic to the crumbs and also slice a tomato or two over the top of the pie before baking.

You can stretch the recipe by adding more eggs and mushrooms; it is designed for those 1¾lb/800g packs of frozen fish fillet in supermarkets but you can of course use fresh fish fillet. You can make the filling in advance and leave just the final baking for the last minute.

For 6–8

- 1¾lb/800g frozen white fish fillet
- 1 pint/570ml milk
- 2oz/50g margarine or butter
- 1 large onion, chopped
- 2 Tbsp plain flour
- 1 Tbsp tomato ketchup or purée
- salt and pepper
- 4–6 hard-boiled eggs
- 2oz/50g butter
- 8–10oz/225–275g mushrooms, quartered or sliced thickly
- 2 tomatoes, sliced (optional)
- 2oz/50g fresh brown or white breadcrumbs
- 1 clove garlic, crushed

For 20

- 3 × 1¾lb/800g frozen white fish fillet
- 3 pints/1.8 litres milk
- 4oz/100g margarine or butter
- 3 large onions, chopped
- 4 Tbsp plain flour
- 3 Tbsp tomato ketchup or purée
- salt and pepper
- 12 hard-boiled eggs
- 6oz/175g butter
- 1½lb/700g mushrooms, quartered or sliced thickly
- 6 tomatoes, sliced (optional)
- 6oz/175g fresh brown or white breadcrumbs
- 2 cloves garlic, crushed

2–3 Tbsp oil for frying crumbs (sunflower or olive)	5–6 Tbsp oil for frying crumbs (sunflower or olive)

Put the fish in a large saucepan, cover with the milk and simmer till just cooked – 10–15 minutes. Hard-boil your eggs now if you haven't already. Use a draining spoon to take the fish from the pan; remove any skin or bones and flake the fish into a large bowl.

Melt the margarine or butter in another large pan and soften the onion in it. Stir in the flour and gradually add the fishy milk to make a smooth sauce, stirring all the time. Stir in the ketchup or purée and season well with salt and pepper. Leave to cook very gently while you cut up the mushrooms and sauté them with the butter in a small covered pan. Preheat the oven to Gas 4/350F/180C.

Remove the pan with the sauce from the heat, stir in the fish, quarter the eggs and add them and finally stir in the mushrooms with their juice. Check the seasoning, then pour the whole lot into a large buttered pie dish; if you are using tomatoes, place the slices over the top of the pie. Bake in the oven for about 30 minutes.

Just before serving, fry the breadcrumbs with the crushed garlic in the oil until golden and crisp, spread them sizzling over the hot pie and serve straight away.

RATATOUILLE WITH EGGS

See pages 181–2 for the Ratatouille recipe.

Allow 1–2 free-range eggs per person.

Put 2 large spoonfuls of the ratatouille per person in a fireproof dish, break the eggs on top and bake, uncovered, in a moderate oven for 5–10 minutes, until the egg whites are just set. A very useful way to feed a few vegetarians among meat-eaters who can have the ratatouille as a vegetable at the same meal.

Puddings

APPLE CURD TART

This simple but delicious recipe comes from another clergy wife, Becky, and is best served warm, as most egg mixtures are. The better flavoured the apples, the better the tart.

You need either a large deep flan tin (11in/28cm across and 2in/5cm deep) or 2 normal-sized ones (9in/23cm across and 1in/2.5cm deep). A Kenwood mixer or other processor is useful for this quantity of pastry.

For 10–12

For the pastry

12oz/350g plain flour
a pinch of salt
6oz/175g butter or butter and lard
3–6 Tbsp cold water

Put the flour and salt in the bowl of the Kenwood, add the fat cut into pieces and mix at speed until it looks like breadcrumbs. Turn the speed down and add just enough water to bring the crumbs into a dough. Switch off, remove the dough and roll out onto a floured board. Butter the tins and line them with the pastry.

For the filling

8oz/225g butter
8oz/225g granulated sugar
4 cooking apples, peeled, cored and grated
4 eggs, lightly beaten

Preheat the oven to Gas 6/400F/200C.

Melt the butter and sugar together in a saucepan. Remove from the heat, mix in the grated apple and the beaten eggs. Tip it all into the pastry case (no pre-baking necessary) and bake for 30–45 minutes (the shorter time for 9in/23cm tins, the longer for 11in/28cm one), until the filling is set.

TROPICAL FRUIT COMPÔTE

! needs to stand overnight

Dried fruit soaked in tea or juice or rose water makes a very good refreshing salad among the puddings or on the breakfast table (see recipe on page 201). This party version, with exotic fruit, tea, honey and spices, comes from Toni Tolhurst, and will serve 8 or more alongside other puddings.

For 8 or more

1 × ¾ pint/400ml Fairtrade orange juice
juice of 1 lime or lemon
2 Fairtrade Earl Grey/Assam teabags
5oz/150g Fairtrade dried mango slices
3½oz/100g Fairtrade dried pineapple pieces
3½oz/100g Fairtrade dried apricots, halved
2–4oz/50–100g Fairtrade raisins (or figs or dates)
2 tsp Fairtrade honey
1 tsp ground mixed spice
1 tsp ground cinnamon
crème fraîche or Greek yogurt to serve

Pour orange and lime or lemon juice into a large saucepan. Add the teabags, bring to the boil and stir. Remove from the heat, add the dried fruits and leave to soak for 30 minutes. Remove the teabags and add the honey and spices. Bring to the boil again and simmer for 15 minutes, then decant carefully into a deep serving bowl and allow to cool overnight.

APRICOT OR PRUNE MOUSSE

! overnight soaking needed

These dried fruit mousses make very good winter puddings – they freeze well too, so can be made in advance. A good use for spare egg whites.

For 10–12

1lb/450g Fairtrade dried apricots
12fl oz/350ml Fairtrade orange juice
3 Tbsp apricot brandy (optional)
½ pint/280ml whipping cream
6 egg whites

or

1lb/450g dried stoneless prunes
12fl oz/350ml cold Fairtrade tea
3 Tbsp port (optional)
½ pint/280ml whipping cream
6 egg whites

Soak the dried fruit in the juice or tea overnight in a saucepan. Next day, bring to the boil and simmer until soft, adding a little water if need be. Whiz to a purée in the liquidiser and add the alcohol if used. You should have a purée of dropping consistency. Whip the cream until it is the same thickness as the purée and fold into the fruit.

Finally whip the egg whites, not too stiffly, and fold them in. Turn into a pretty bowl and keep refrigerated.

SPRINGFIELD PEAR CAKE

This most excellent upside-down pear cake recipe comes from Jane Grigson's *Fruit Book* (Penguin 1983) and is the pudding our family most hope for at Sunday lunches. The ginger flavouring and buttery cake mixture combine with the pear to make a superb pudding. You need a shallow cake tin or small roasting pan measuring 8 × 12in/20 × 30cm and 2½in/6cm deep.

For 6–8

For the topping

4oz/110g lightly salted butter, cut up
4oz/110g Fairtrade granulated sugar
3 Tbsp syrup from jar of preserved ginger
4 or 5 large firm pears
juice of a large lemon

For the cake

6oz/150g softened butter
6oz/150g Fairtrade caster sugar or light soft brown sugar
5oz/130g self-raising flour
1½ level tsp baking powder
1½oz/40g ground almonds
3 large eggs
4 Tbsp syrup from a jar of preserved ginger
4 knobs preserved ginger, coarsely chopped

First the topping: take your shallow tin, set it over low heat and put in the butter. Stir about with a wooden spoon, pushing butter up the sides of the tin to grease them. Add the sugar and syrup to make a rich, creamy-fawn bubbling mixture, a pale toffee colour. Remove from the heat.

Preheat the oven to Gas 5/375F/190C. Peel, core and thinly slice the pears, turning them in lemon juice on a plate so they don't discolour. Arrange them decoratively over the toffee base – they will come out as the top of the pudding.

Tip all the cake ingredients, except the chopped ginger, into a mixer or food processor and whiz to smoothness. Or beat everything together with a wooden spoon. Add the ginger and spread over the top of the pears.

Bake in the oven for 45 minutes. If the top is richly brown and well risen, turn the heat down to Gas 4/350F/180C. Leave until the edges of the cake are shrinking from the sides of the tin and a skewer pushed in at an angle comes out clean – about 15 minutes. Remove from the oven and run a knife between the tin and the cake to make sure it won't stick.

Put a deep serving plate over the top, upside down, then turn the whole thing over with one quick movement, protecting your hands with a cloth. Leave for a few minutes with the tin on top to drain all the juices over the cake.

Serve warm or cold, with pouring cream.

COLLETTE'S CHOCOLATE ROULADE

This is the pudding that we have served here more than any other at parties over the years; it is best made by Collette and here is her recipe.

For 10–12

8–10oz/225–275g Fairtrade dark chocolate
5 large free-range eggs
8oz Fairtrade caster sugar
¾ pint/450ml double cream
fruit of your choice – cherries, raspberries – about 1lb/450g
a little icing sugar

Preheat the oven to Gas 5/375F/190C. Lay baking parchment over your largest baking tray and sprinkle with icing sugar.

Melt the chocolate in a small bowl over boiling water, or in the microwave. Separate the eggs, putting the yolks into a bowl large enough to take a whisk. Add the sugar to the yolks and whisk together until they turn pale and leave a trail when you pull out the whisk – the 'ribbon' stage. Stir in the melted chocolate. Whisk the whites in a separate bowl till stiff, then fold them into the chocolate mixture. You will need a second whisk for this, or else wash and dry your whisk very thoroughly.

Spread the roulade mixture over the parchment and bake in the centre of the oven till firm – for about 20 minutes. Remove from the oven and cover with a tea cloth till cool. Whip the cream till it holds its shape – not too thick – and spread it all over the roulade. Spread the fruit over the cream and then roll up from a short end, using the paper to help tip it over.

Serve on a large oval platter.

Note: 1–2oz/30–50g more melted chocolate drizzled over the filling before rolling adds a lovely crunch.

MRS GORONWY'S MARMALADE TART

This is a family favourite, an excellent way to use homemade marmalade. It keeps well for a day or two in the fridge, so can be made in advance.

These quantities will be enough for two 9in/23cm tart tins.

Note: There is no need to pre-bake the pastry if you have an Aga – simply bake the filled tart on the bottom surface of the hot oven.

For 10–12

For the pastry

Shortcrust pastry to line two 9in/23cm tart tins (see Apple Curd Tart recipe, page 36). To pre-bake, fill the cases with scrumpled foil and bake for 10 minutes in a moderate oven (Gas 4/350F/180C).

For the filling

6oz/175g soft margarine
6oz/175g Fairtrade granulated sugar
4 free-range eggs
6 heaped Tbsp bitter marmalade
3oz/80g Fairtrade walnut pieces

Preheat the oven to Gas 5/375F/190C.

Beat all the ingredients, except the walnuts, together until smooth. Pour into the pastry cases and scatter the walnut pieces over the top. Bake until the filling is set and the pastry golden – about 30 minutes.

Serve warm or cold, with cream or without.

VEILED FARMER'S DAUGHTER

This is a name which captures the imagination; the recipe crops up in many variations. The basic idea is that you make layers of fruit, something crunchy and whipped cream – the veil presumably being the final covering layer of cream. Another version uses amaretti, those crisp Italian biscuits, instead of the crumbs and autumn raspberries in place of strawberries. You could use nectarines in the autumn and spiced apple purée in winter – the possibilities are endless. You can either make it in one large bowl or in individual glasses. I think it is often nice to have some individual cups or glasses of jellies or creams among the larger puddings at a buffet.

For 8–10

10–12oz/275–350g wholemeal breadcrumbs
(about 6 large slices)
6 Tbsp Fairtrade demerara sugar
1 tsp cinnamon
1–1½lb/450–700g ripe strawberries or other fruit
a little kirsch or orange liqueur (optional)
¼ pint/150ml double cream
¼ pint/150ml whipping cream
1 Tbsp vanilla sugar

Preheat the oven to Gas 6/400F/200C.

First, mix the breadcrumbs, demerara and cinnamon and spread them on a baking tray in the oven. Bake until crisp – the time will depend on the staleness of the bread, so check every few minutes, stirring the crumbs to dry them out. When crisp and crunchy, remove and allow to cool. See note below.

Wipe and halve or quarter the strawberries and sprinkle with alcohol if used. Whip the creams together into light peaks and whip in the vanilla sugar.

Arrange in layers in the large bowl or individual glasses, first fruit, then cream, then crumbs, ending with cream but keeping back a few crumbs to sprinkle over just before serving. Refrigerate until needed.

Note: You can crisp the crumbs in advance, when the oven is on for something else. Keep them airtight when cold.

RASPBERRY AND GINGER SHORTBREAD 

When I was choosing recipes for this book, David was very anxious that this one should get in. The gingery shortbread goes wonderfully with the raspberries and it is a useful way to stretch the fruit for a party. It comes from Elizabeth David's *Summer Cooking* (Museum Press 1955). Autumn raspberries are just as good, if not better.

For 8–10

2lb/900g raspberries
2–3oz/50–75g Fairtrade caster sugar
12oz/350g plain flour
1 tsp ground ginger
2 tsp baking powder
7oz/190g Fairtrade light muscovado sugar
4oz/110g butter

Preheat the oven to Gas 4/350F/180C.

Spread the raspberries in a large shallow ovenproof dish and strew them with caster sugar. Put all the dry ingredients into a mixer bowl and blend or rub in the butter, cut in small pieces. When it looks like breadcrumbs, spread it over the fruit and smooth it out without pressing it down.

Bake in the middle of the oven for 25–30 minutes, until pale gold and crisping at the edges. Serve hot or cold.

Winter

December, January, February

The days are closing in and warming soups are called for. Christmas and New Year festivities take over the kitchen and then we are into the coldest part of the year, needing hot meals to cheer us on. Baked or mashed potato and spicy red cabbage go well with winter stews and chocolate puddings come into their own.

Winter

Soups

Mushroom Soup
Apple and Chestnut Soup
Stilton Soup
Curried Parsnip Soup
Tuscan Minestrone
Leek and Potato Soup (and Crème Vichyssoise)
Garlic and Bread Soup

Main Courses

Medallions of Pork with Orange and Ginger
L'Estouffat de Boeuf (Beef Stew)
Bacon and Lentils
Salmi of Game or Turkey
V Cheesy Parsnip Bake
V Butterbean and Leek Gratin
V Hilary's Savoury Bean Pot
V Christmas Nut Wellington
V Vegetable Khichdi
Fish and Fennel Lasagne

Puddings

Hot Chocolate Sauce Pudding
Pears Baked in Wine
Caramel Oranges
Chocolate Crunch Christmas Pudding
Elizabeth Raffald's Orange Custards
Rolled Lemon Cream
Chestnut and Chocolate Cake
Blackcurrant Parfait

Soups

MUSHROOM SOUP

Mushrooms are available all the year around and they make a good warming winter soup. Large open mushrooms have a stronger flavour than small button ones. This soup freezes well.

For 6–8	*For 20*
2oz/50g butter	6oz/175g butter
1lb/450g mushrooms, finely sliced	2½lb/1.2kg mushrooms, finely sliced
1 heaped Tbsp flour	3 heaped Tbsp flour
2½ pints/1.5 litres chicken or vegetable stock	6 pints/3.5 litres chicken or vegetable stock
¾ pint/425ml milk	2 pints/1.2 litres milk
salt and pepper	salt and pepper
a squeeze of lemon juice	juice of one lemon
3 Tbsp single cream	¼ pint/150ml single cream
finely chopped parsley	finely chopped parsley

Melt the butter in a large saucepan and sweat the mushrooms in it, covered, for 5–10 minutes. Add the flour, stir to absorb the butter and season with a grind of pepper. Add the stock gradually, stirring, and simmer for 20–30 minutes, then add the milk and cook for 10 minutes more.

Liquidise, in batches if need be, return to the pan, taste and season. This is the stage to freeze it if convenient.

Reheat in the pan, add the lemon juice, which intensifies the mushroom flavour, stir in the cream and parsley to serve.

APPLE AND CHESTNUT SOUP

! overnight soaking needed if dried chestnuts used

This chestnut soup is unusual for the addition of apple, which lightens the texture and the flavour. Fresh chestnuts need to be slit, boiled or baked and peeled before use; if you haven't time for that, dried chestnuts, soaked overnight and boiled until tender, or else tinned unsweetened whole chestnuts can perfectly well be used, though the tinned option will be more expensive.

The recipe comes from a small book of apple recipes, *Cooking Apples*, published for Ampleforth Abbey (in North Yorkshire) by Gracewing in 1982.

For 6–8	*For 20*
2lb/900g fresh chestnuts, peeled (see above)	4½lb/2kg fresh chestnuts, peeled (see above)
or 1lb/450g dried chestnuts, soaked and cooked	*or* 2lb/1kg dried chestnuts, soaked and cooked
or 2 × 1lb/450g tins whole unsweetened chestnuts	*or* 4 × 1lb/450g tins whole unsweetened chestnuts
2 sticks celery, chopped	4 sticks celery, chopped
4 pints/2.4 litres light stock or water	8 pints/5 litres light stock or water
4 large dessert apples (Cox or Reinette), peeled, cored and sliced	8 large dessert apples (Cox or Reinette), peeled, cored and sliced
3oz/75g butter	6oz/150g butter
salt and pepper	salt and pepper
¼ pint/150ml single cream	½ pint/280ml single cream
croûtons (optional)	croûtons (optional)

Put the chestnuts and chopped celery in a large pan with half the stock, bring to the boil, cover and simmer until the chestnuts and celery are soft – about 20 minutes.

Meanwhile, melt the butter in a small pan and cook the apple pieces in it with a little salt and pepper.

When both chestnuts and apples are soft, liquidise together, return to the big pan and dilute with the rest of the stock until it is the consistency you like. Check and adjust the seasoning and stir in the cream just before serving, with the croûtons alongside, if used (see page 202).

STILTON SOUP

Stilton is one of the best leftovers after Christmas, to be used in soup or in Locket's Savoury (see page 101). This soup is quite rich, so serve in small bowls.

For 6–8	*For 20*
2oz/50g butter	5oz/150g butter
3 medium onions, chopped	7 medium onions, chopped
2 Tbsp flour	4 Tbsp flour
1½ pints/850ml milk	3½ pints/2.2 litres milk
4oz/120g Stilton cheese	10–12oz/300–350g Stilton cheese
5fl oz/150ml double cream	½–1 pint/280–570ml double cream
salt and pepper	salt and pepper
chives, chopped	chives, chopped

Melt the butter in a large pan, add the onion and stir over gentle heat until golden and soft. Sprinkle in the flour and mix to absorb the butter. Stir the milk in gradually and bring to the boil. Cover and simmer for 30–40 minutes (very gently so it doesn't boil over).

Crumble in the Stilton so that it melts into the soup. Stir in the cream, taste and season with salt and pepper. Sprinkle the chives on top as you serve it.

CURRIED PARSNIP SOUP

I make no apology for including a version of Jane Grigson's wonderful curried parsnip soup; it has become a classic and can appear in its grandest form (real beef stock and plenty of cream) for dinner parties or in a more frugal form (stock cubes or vegetable stock and less cream) at Lent lunches. The curry powder specified betrays its 1970s origins; you may prefer to use curry paste, but don't overdo the curry flavour.

For 6–8	*For 20*
3oz/80g butter	6oz/150g butter
1 large parsnip, peeled and sliced	3–4 large parsnips, peeled and sliced
4oz/120g onion, chopped	12oz/350g onion, chopped
1 clove garlic, crushed	2 cloves garlic, crushed
1 Tbsp flour	3 Tbsp flour
1 rounded tsp curry powder or paste	2–3 rounded tsp curry powder or paste
2 pints/1.2 litres hot beef stock or vegetable stock	6 pints/3.6 litres hot beef stock or vegetable stock
salt and pepper	salt and pepper
¼ pint/150ml single cream	½ pint/280ml single cream
chives	chives
croûtons (optional)	croûtons (optional)

Melt the butter in a heavy saucepan and add the parsnip, onion and garlic. Cover and cook them gently in the butter for 10 minutes or so, stirring once or twice to make sure they don't brown. Add the flour and the curry powder or paste and stir to absorb the butter.

Then gradually add the hot stock, stirring as you go until all is in. Cover and simmer until the parsnip is soft – about 20 minutes. Liquidise, in batches if necessary, return to the pan, taste and adjust the seasoning.

Before serving, stir in the cream and sprinkle with chopped chives. Croûtons (see page 202) are nice but not vital.

TUSCAN MINESTRONE

! overnight soaking needed

One bowl is a complete meal.

This is classic Italian peasant food, a minestrone with bacon to enrich it and beans, potatoes and pasta to fill you up. If you are feeding vegetarians, omit the bacon and provide extra cheese. The vegetables can of course be varied with the season – this is a winter version. Before embarking on this soup, make sure you have enough large soup bowls to serve it in. Small ones won't do. Borrow some if need be. If you haven't got Parmesan in a chunk, use freshly grated mature Cheddar instead; it will taste better than dusty, ready-grated Parmesan.

For 6–8	*For 20*
½lb/225g dried white beans (haricot or cannellini), soaked overnight	1½lb/700g dried white beans (haricot or cannellini), soaked overnight
3 Tbsp olive oil	6 Tbsp olive oil
3 onions, sliced	6 onions, sliced
3 cloves garlic, halved	6 cloves garlic, halved
4oz/120g pancetta or streaky bacon, cut small	6–8oz/175g–225g pancetta or streaky bacon, cut small
4 large tomatoes, chopped (or 1 × 14oz/400g tin)	8 large tomatoes, chopped (or 2 × 14oz/400g tins)
1 glass red wine	2 glasses red wine
4 pints/2.4 litres hot water	8 pints/4.8 litres hot water
a large bunch of parsley, thyme and sage	a large bunch of parsley, thyme and sage
3 large carrots, diced	6 large carrots, diced
3 medium potatoes, diced	6 medium potatoes, diced
3 sticks of celery, chopped	6 sticks of celery, chopped

½ small Savoy cabbage, sliced finely	1 small Savoy cabbage, sliced finely
3oz/80g small pasta shapes or broken spaghetti	6oz/175g small pasta shapes or broken spaghetti
salt and pepper	salt and pepper
1–2oz/25–50g Parmesan, to grate	3–6oz/80–175g Parmesan, to grate

Heat the oil in a large pan, melt the onions in it, adding the garlic and bacon; stir around until the onions are soft. Then add the chopped tomatoes and pour in the wine to bubble for a few minutes before adding the drained beans; lay in the bunch of herbs and cover with hot water, bring to the boil and cook steadily for about 2 hours, until the beans are soft. *Do not add salt before the beans are done.* Then add the carrots, potatoes and celery, add salt to taste and cook for 20 minutes or so before finally adding the cabbage and pasta, which will only need 5–10 minutes to cook. Check the seasoning, stir in 3 tablespoons of grated cheese and serve the rest of the grated cheese separately.

Serve crusty bread with the soup – the Tuscans would break pieces of bread into it to thicken it more.

LEEK AND POTATO SOUP (AND CRÈME VICHYSSOISE)

Leeks and potatoes feature large in the winter and combine to make one of the best soups there is. If you grow leeks and have a winter glut, you may like to make extra amounts of the basic soup, freeze it before adding the milk and use it in the summer for that deliciously creamy iced soup Vichyssoise.

For 6–8	*For 20*
3oz/80g butter	6oz/175g butter
4 large leeks, trimmed and sliced	8–10 large leeks, trimmed and sliced
2 small onions, chopped	4 small onions, chopped
2 pints/1.2 litres water or light stock	4½ pints/2.5 litres water or light stock
1lb/450g potatoes, peeled and diced	2½lb/1kg potatoes, peeled and diced
salt	salt
¾ pint/425ml milk	2 pints/1.2 litres milk
For hot soup	*For hot soup*
1 Tbsp cream or knob of butter	3 Tbsp cream or 2oz/50g butter
croûtons (optional)	croûtons (optional)
For iced Crème Vichyssoise	*For iced Crème Vichyssoise*
½ pint/280ml single cream	1 pint/570ml single cream
¼ pint/140ml double cream	½ pint/280ml double cream
chives, finely chopped	chives, finely chopped

Melt the butter in a large heavy pan, add the leeks and onions, cover and sweat them gently for 5–10 minutes, not letting them brown.

Add the water or stock and the diced potatoes and salt to taste. Cover and simmer until the potatoes are soft. Liquidise, in batches if need be. (Freeze at this stage if you are keeping it for summer.)

For the hot version, heat the milk and add it to the soup, bringing it all to just under the boil. Taste and add more salt if necessary. Stir in the cream or an extra knob of butter and serve with croûtons (see page 202) if you like.

For Crème Vichyssoise, defrost the basic purée, heat and add the milk and single cream. Bring nearly to the boil, stirring to prevent it catching. Liquidise again for a super-smooth soup, stir in the double cream, check the seasoning and chill thoroughly. Serve sprinkled with finely chopped chives.

GARLIC AND BREAD SOUP

There's something very cleansing about garlic soup, especially at the end of a season of rich food, like Christmas – you can feel it doing you good. Actually it tastes good too. This is a simple version, with no added fat (even better for you) but it does need really good stock, preferably a light homemade chicken or vegetable one (see page 216). If you have to use stock cubes or powder, buy the best quality you can find and make allowance for their saltiness when you season.

For 6–8

4 pints/2.4 litres good stock, chicken or vegetable
24 fat cloves garlic (2–3 heads), peeled
salt, black pepper, nutmeg
4–6 thick slices stale white bread, crusts and all, cubed

Heat up the stock in a large pan, put the peeled cloves of garlic in, bring to the boil, cover and simmer for 30–40 minutes. When the garlic is really soft, fish out with a slotted spoon and liquidise with a ladleful of hot soup. Return to the pan, stir and taste. Adjust the seasoning with salt, black pepper and grated nutmeg.

Add the cubes of bread and leave to disintegrate and thicken the soup.

This is not a party soup; serve by the fireside in warm bowls with a glass of good red wine.

You can enrich this very simple formula by stirring in a tablespoon of olive oil or a couple of eggs beaten with a spoonful of olive oil. If you do add eggs, make sure the soup doesn't boil again.

Main Courses

MEDALLIONS OF PORK WITH ORANGE AND GINGER

I cannot pretend that pork fillets are cheap but they are economical with one's own time for preparation and with the time needed for cooking. This is a delicious party recipe, served recently in Wolvesey Castle in Winchester to a gathering of bishops. I find one 12oz/350g fillet feeds 2–3; that night at Wolvesey, 8 of us consumed 6 fillets. Allow at least 5oz/150g pork each.

You will need two large frying pans to cope with the larger amount.

For 6–8	*For 20*
3–4 pork fillets, weighing 2½lb/1.2kg	5lb/2.25kg pork fillets
3 oranges	6 oranges
3oz/80g butter	6oz/175g butter
4oz/120g Fairtrade brown sugar	8oz/225g Fairtrade brown sugar
2 Tbsp syrup from jar of preserved ginger	4 Tbsp syrup from jar of preserved ginger
1½ Tbsp cornflour	3 Tbsp cornflour
6 Tbsp wine vinegar, red or white	10–12 Tbsp wine vinegar, red or white
¼–½ pint/150–280ml light stock (from chicken stock cube)	½–1 pint/280–570ml light stock (from chicken stock cube)

salt and pepper	salt and pepper
1–2oz/25–50g preserved ginger, thinly sliced	2–3oz/50–75g preserved ginger, thinly sliced
1 orange, peeled and sliced, to serve	2 oranges, peeled and sliced, to serve

First, cut the fillets into 1in/2.5cm thick pieces, lay them flat on a board, cover with clingfilm or greaseproof paper and bash them with a rolling pin to flatten to about ¼in/5mm thick – not paper thin.

Use a potato peeler to pare the peel from one orange and cut it into thin strips. Squeeze the juice from all the oranges.

Fry the beaten slices of pork in butter on both sides till *lightly* browned. Set aside in the serving dish and keep warm.

Mix together the orange juice, sugar, ginger syrup, cornflour, vinegar and a little of the stock and pour into the frying pan. Bring to the boil and simmer for 2 minutes to thicken. Taste and season with salt and pepper. Add the orange peel strips and ginger and cook for a further 2 minutes.

Pour over the pork and serve immediately, *or* cool and freeze. Garnish with slices of orange.

L'ESTOUFFAT DE BOEUF (BEEF STEW) ☺

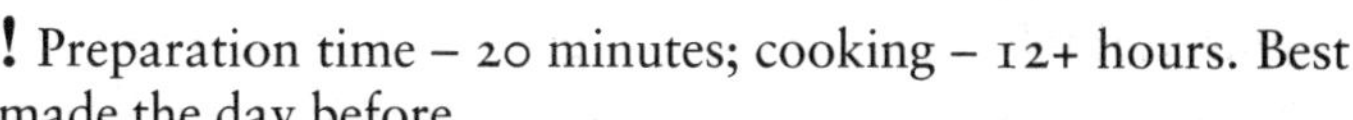

! Preparation time – 20 minutes; cooking – 12+ hours. Best made the day before.

Most of us serve traditional fare on Christmas Day which we vary at our peril; the advantage to the cook is that we don't have to think and choose too much, just get on and do it. But around Christmas Day, before and after, we are likely to have plenty of mouths to feed and can be more adventurous.

Here is a very simple beef daube, described by Elizabeth David in *French Country Cooking* (John Lehmann 1951) as traditional Gascon fare for Christmas Eve. These quantities will feed 10–12 people – if you are fewer, do make the whole amount because it reheats beautifully, or is delicious cold a few days later. You need a heavy casserole, preferably oval, which will neatly fit the meat.

For 10–12

1½lb/700g fresh pork rind *or* a pig's foot, split
(ask the butcher)
6lb/2.7kg beef topside in one long piece
salt and pepper
8 shallots or small whole onions
2 large onions, quartered
2 carrots, cut in half
bouquet garni of parsley, thyme and bay leaf tied together
3–4fl oz/75–100ml Armagnac or brandy
half a bottle of robust red wine

Put the pork rind or pig's foot at the bottom of the casserole, season the beef all over with salt and pepper and lay it on top. Tuck the vegetables and the bouquet garni in all around and pour the Armagnac over, then the wine, which should just cover the meat.

Preheat the oven to Gas 1/275F/140C.

Cover the casserole and heat gently on top of the stove, bringing it slowly to a simmer. Then transfer to the oven and leave for 10–12 hours, or overnight. Remove from the oven to a cool place. Remove the cooled fat from the top. Retrieve the pork rind from under the beef and cut up into small squares. Discard the vegetables and reheat the whole thing gently to serve.

Cook fresh vegetables to go with the Estouffat – perhaps buttered parsnips or glazed carrots and baked potatoes.

Note: If you have to fit your meat into a round casserole, you will probably need to cut it into two; the important thing is to have it fitting closely, so that once the vegetables are in you don't need too much wine to cover it.

BACON AND LENTILS

An easy, economical, sustaining dish which we often have on Christmas Eve is this combination of bacon and lentils. Don't waste the best gammon on this; a piece of collar will do very well. The initial boiling and draining of the bacon saves you from soaking it overnight. To feed more people, add more lentils.

For 6–8

about 2lb/1kg piece of bacon
1½oz/35g lard or vegetable oil
12 small onions, peeled, or 3 large, quartered
black pepper
1lb/450g continental lentils
1 large carrot, cut in two
1 stick celery
bouquet garni of thyme, parsley and bay leaf tied together
2–3 garlic cloves, crushed
butter and parsley to serve

Put the bacon into a large saucepan, cover with water and bring to the boil, drain and rinse in cold water and dry with kitchen paper.

Melt the fat in a large casserole, put in the bacon and onions with a grind or two of black pepper. When the onions begin to brown, add the lentils, carrot and celery and the bouquet garni. Cover with water and a lid and bring to the boil and cook very gently for about 2 hours.

Remove the bacon, vegetables and herbs and strain the lentils (keep the liquid for making soup). Put the lentils onto a warmed serving dish with a lump of butter stirred in, cut the bacon in slices and arrange them around the lentils and garnish it all with chopped parsley.

Serve with baked potatoes and salad.

SALMI OF GAME OR TURKEY

A good way of using up leftover game or even the everlasting turkey is to reheat slices of the meat in a strongly flavoured wine sauce, with mushrooms to moisten it. It's a medieval idea, passed on to us by Jane Grigson in her *English Food* (Macmillan 1974), and very good indeed.

For 6–8

leftover game or turkey, preferably not overcooked;
  aim at about 1½lb/700g meat off the bone
¾ pint/425ml stock made from the carcass
2oz/50g butter
3 shallots or 2 small onions, chopped
1 heaped Tbsp flour
bouquet garni of bay leaf, parsley and thyme tied together
thinly pared peel of an orange, preferably Seville
  (use a potato peeler)
salt, pepper, lemon juice
¼ pint/150ml red (or white) wine
¼lb/125g button mushrooms, fried in butter
orange quarters (sweet, not Seville) and croûtons to serve

First take the meat off the bone (if it's turkey, try to get dark as well as white meat) and use the bones to make the stock (boil with water, herbs, a small carrot, salt and pepper, an onion, 2 cloves of garlic for 30 minutes).

Melt the butter in a medium-sized saucepan and cook the shallots or onion until a rich golden colour. Stir in the flour and add the strained stock gradually. Simmer for 20–30 minutes with the bouquet garni and orange peel until the sauce is quite well thickened.

Strain through a sieve into a shallow casserole, season to taste with salt, pepper and lemon juice and add the wine and fried mushrooms with their juices. Simmer for 5 minutes, then add the meat slices, cover and leave to heat through for 10 or 20 minutes. Don't let it boil again. Tuck croûtons (see page 202) round the edge and garnish with orange quarters.

CHEESY PARSNIP BAKE

Parsnips roast and mash well and are good just buttered. Here is a favourite supper dish; potatoes bulk out the parsnips for large numbers. Choose mature cheese.

For 6–8

2½lb/1.2kg parsnips, cut up
3–4oz/100–125g butter
8oz/225g mature Cheddar, grated
salt and pepper

For 20

5lb/2.4kg parsnips, cut up
2½lb/1.2kg potatoes, cut up small
6–8oz/190–225g butter
1lb/450g mature Cheddar, grated
salt and pepper

Preheat the oven to Gas 5/375F/190C.

Bring the parsnips (and potatoes) to the boil in a pan of salted water, cover and cook until tender, for about 20 minutes. Drain and mash the vegetables with the butter, season with pepper and then beat in half the grated cheese. Taste and add more salt if need be.

Put into a well-buttered pie dish and sprinkle on the rest of the cheese.

Bake in the oven for 20–30 minutes and serve with beef or sausages for meat-eaters, or in its own right with baked tomatoes and baked eggs alongside.

BUTTERBEAN AND LEEK GRATIN

! overnight soaking needed

This bean and vegetable gratin is fairly simple but tasty and sustaining. You could serve it with steamed root vegetables or just crusty bread and a salad. It comes from Rosamond Richardson's *Complete Vegetarian Cooking* (Sainsbury 1991).

For 6–8	*For 20*
12oz/350g dried butterbeans, soaked overnight	1½lb/700g dried butterbeans, soaked overnight
4 leeks, chopped	8 leeks, chopped
½ large cauliflower, broken into florets	1 large cauliflower, broken into florets
2oz/50g butter or margarine	4oz/120g butter or margarine
1 medium onion, chopped	2 large onions, chopped
3 cloves garlic, chopped	5 cloves garlic, chopped
2 scant Tbsp plain flour	4 Tbsp plain flour
2 tsp coriander seeds, ground	3 tsp coriander seeds, ground
2 Tbsp grainy mustard	3 Tbsp grainy mustard
2 tsp clear honey	3–4 tsp clear honey
5 Tbsp single cream (optional)	8 Tbsp single cream (optional)
3oz/80g mature Cheddar, grated	6oz/170g mature Cheddar, grated
6oz/170g fresh breadcrumbs – brown, white or a mixture	12oz/350g fresh breadcrumbs – brown, white or a mixture
salt and pepper	salt and pepper

Drain and rinse the soaked beans, put them in a saucepan and cover generously with water. Bring to the boil, cover and simmer for 45–55 minutes, until tender. Drain, reserving the liquid.

Meanwhile, bring another pan of water to the boil, salt lightly and cook the leeks and cauliflower in it for just 5 minutes. Drain well, reserving the water, and set aside.

Melt the butter or margarine in a large pan, add the onion and garlic and cook for 5–8 minutes, till soft. Sprinkle in the flour and stir to absorb the fat. Add the coriander and season with salt and pepper, add about ½ pint/280ml of the vegetable water, stirring all the time to make a smooth sauce. If it is too thick, use some of the bean water to slacken it. Stir in the mustard and honey and cook over a low heat for 10 minutes or so.

Preheat the oven to Gas 4/350F/180C.

Add the leeks and cauliflower to the sauce and stir in with the cream if used. Taste and season again. Put it all in an ovenproof gratin dish (see note below).

Mix the cheese and breadcrumbs together, sprinkle over the top and bake for 30 minutes, till golden, crisp and bubbling.

Note: You can do all the preparation in advance, up to the final addition of breadcrumbs and cheese, cool and keep it in the fridge until half an hour before the party, then continue with the topping and baking.

HILARY'S SAVOURY BEAN POT

! overnight soaking needed if dried beans used

This bean casserole is vegetable food at its best – so tasty that meat-eaters want it too. The recipe came from an American friend, and the sugar and vinegar involved speak of American origins. Quite a lot of chopping and grating, so those with food processors will be at an advantage.

For 6–8	*For 20*
1lb/450g dried red kidney beans, soaked and cooked	2½lb/450g dried red kidney beans, soaked and cooked
or 2 × 14oz/400g tins cooked red kidney beans	*or* 5–6 × 14oz/400g tins cooked red kidney beans
3 Tbsp vegetable oil	6 Tbsp vegetable oil
2 vegetable stock cubes, crumbled	3–4 vegetable stock cubes, crumbled
3 medium onions, chopped	7 medium onions, chopped
3 eating apples, peeled and grated	7 eating apples, peeled and grated
3 medium carrots, grated	7 medium carrots, grated
4 Tbsp tomato purée	8 Tbsp tomato purée
¾ pint/425ml water	2½ pints/1.5 litres water
2–3 Tbsp white wine vinegar or cider vinegar	4 Tbsp white wine vinegar or cider vinegar
1 Tbsp dried English mustard	2 Tbsp dried English mustard
1½ tsp dried oregano	1 Tbsp dried oregano
1½ tsp ground cumin	1 Tbsp ground cumin
1 Tbsp Fairtrade dark brown sugar	2 Tbsp Fairtrade dark brown sugar
salt and pepper	salt and pepper
a little yogurt, sour cream or crème fraîche to serve	a little yogurt, sour cream or crème fraîche to serve

Preheat the oven to Gas 4/350F/180C.

Take a heavy casserole large enough to fit everything. Heat the oil in it and add the crumbled stock cubes, onions, apples and carrots. Sauté for 5 minutes, stirring to prevent sticking. Add the tomato purée with the water and all other flavourings, stirring well.

Finally add the drained cooked beans. Cover and cook in the oven for 35–40 minutes. Inspect halfway through and add a little more water if need be.

Serve topped with swirls of yogurt, sour cream or crème fraîche, with baked potatoes or rice and a salad.

CHRISTMAS NUT WELLINGTON

This makes a very good Christmas treat for vegetarians, and the traditional Christmas vegetables, such as sprouts, red cabbage and roast potatoes would go well with it. I give quantities for a 2lb/1kg loaf tin, which feeds 6 generously; if you have a second tin you can easily double the recipe.

For 6–8

12oz–1lb/350–400g puff pastry
1 small onion, chopped
2 sticks celery, chopped
1 clove garlic, chopped
1 Tbsp sunflower oil and a little more for frying
4oz/110g Fairtrade walnuts
4oz/110g Fairtrade cashews
6oz/175g chestnut purée, unsweetened
1 heaped tsp paprika
1 tsp dried oregano
2 Tbsp fresh lemon juice
2 free-range eggs, beaten
salt and pepper
2oz/50g mushrooms, sliced
beaten egg to glaze

Preheat the oven to Gas 7/425F/220C.

Roll out the pastry on a lightly floured surface. Use most of it to line an oiled 2lb/1kg loaf tin, leaving enough overlapping to fold over and cover the top. Keep back a little pastry for decoration.

Fry the onion, celery and garlic in a little oil. Put into a bowl with the tablespoon of oil, the walnuts, cashews, chestnut purée, paprika, oregano, lemon juice and seasoning. Mix well and bind it with the beaten eggs. Taste and adjust the seasoning.

Lay the mushrooms in the bottom of the pastry-lined tin. Fill it with the nut mixture, pushing down firmly among the mushrooms. Brush the loose edges of the pastry with beaten egg and cover the pie by bringing the pastry up and over, pressing the edges to seal. Place an oiled baking sheet on top of the tin, tip it over and take the tin off the loaf.

Use the spare pastry to make suitable decorations – holly leaves maybe – and stick them on with beaten egg. Make some diagonal cuts to allow steam to escape, brush the whole thing with more beaten egg to glaze and put it in the oven.

Bake for an hour, reducing the temperature halfway through to Gas 4/350F/180C.

Serve hot, though it's also good cold.

VEGETABLE KHICHDI

This Indian recipe comes from a Fairtrade calendar and went down well at a Bishop's Council supper; it really is an all-in-one meal, tasty and satisfying.

For 6–8	*For 20*
8oz/225g red lentils	1¼lb/600g red lentils
2 Tbsp oil	5 Tbsp oil
4 medium onions, finely chopped	8 medium onions, finely chopped
12oz/350g Fairtrade basmati rice	1¾lb/800g Fairtrade basmati rice
6oz/150g peas (frozen are fine)	1lb/450g peas (frozen are fine)
6 medium potatoes, peeled and chopped fine	3lb/1.3kg potatoes, peeled and chopped fine
6oz/150g cauliflower, finely chopped	1lb/450g cauliflower, finely chopped
1 tsp cumin seeds	3 tsp cumin seeds
1in/2.5cm piece cinnamon stick	2–3in/5–7cm piece cinnamon stick
4 cloves	6 cloves
3 cardamom pods	5 cardamom pods
1–2 tsp chilli powder	3–4 tsp chilli powder
2 cloves garlic	4 cloves garlic
boiling water	boiling water
salt	salt

Soak the lentils in boiling water for 10 minutes. Meanwhile, heat the oil in a large pan and fry the onions until they begin to brown. Add the rice and drained lentils, vegetables, spices and garlic. Continue to stir fry until the rice sticks.

Pour in boiling water to cover, season with salt and mix well. Cover the pan, bring to the boil and simmer for 10–15 minutes, until the rice, lentils and vegetables are all cooked and the liquid absorbed. Taste and adjust the seasoning before serving.

Note: Vary the vegetables according to the season – carrots, courgettes, green beans could all be used – but I think there should always be peas and potatoes. You can use continental lentils instead of red, in which case part cook them first.

FISH AND FENNEL LASAGNE

Staff lunches come round once a month – simple but sustaining food for 10–12 people. Luckily our vegetarian archdeacon does eat fish; this lasagne was created for a February meeting, when fennel bulbs were to be had in the market and the fish stall was well stocked. You can vary the fish, of course; this mixture of white and smoked and prawns makes for a complex and interesting taste.

You could use the same recipe for a fish pie, omitting the lasagne and covering the fish mixture with mashed potato, or potato and celeriac mashed together.

For 6–8	*For 20*
2lb/900g mixed fish fillet (1½lb/700g white to ½lb/225g smoked)	6lb/2.7kg mixed fish fillet (5lb/2.3kg white to 1lb/450g smoked)
¼lb/120g prawns, peeled	½lb/240g prawns, peeled
2 pints/1.2 litres milk	6 pints/3.6 litres milk
1 large fennel bulb	3 large fennel bulbs
1oz/25g butter	3oz/75g butter
juice of ½ lemon	juice of 1 large lemon
3oz/75g more butter	8oz/200g more butter
2 heaped Tbsp flour	6 heaped Tbsp flour
salt and pepper	salt and pepper
1lb/450g lasagne sheets, plain or green	3lb/350g lasagne sheets, plain or green
1–2oz/25–50g grated cheese (Parmesan and Cheddar)	4–6oz/120–175g grated cheese (Parmesan and Cheddar)

Preheat the oven to Gas 4/350F/180C.

Lay the fish in a wide, well-buttered ovenproof dish, season with salt and pepper and cover generously with about half the milk. Use foil or a lid to cover the dish and bake in the oven for around 20 minutes, until the fish is just cooked.

Meanwhile, wash the fennel and cut into small chunky pieces. Put these in a smaller ovenproof dish or casserole with the 1oz/25g of butter and the lemon juice. Cover and put in the oven to cook for 20 minutes or until tender, shaking or stirring once or twice.

Note: If you haven't an Aga and don't want to keep your oven on for too long, you can do this preliminary cooking of fish and fennel on top of the stove, gently so as not to burn butter or milk.

When the fish is cooked, lift it out, skin and flake, removing any stray bones, and put into a large bowl.

When the fennel pieces are done add them to the fish, keeping the juice to enliven the sauce.

Melt the 3oz/75g butter in a saucepan, add the flour and use the remaining milk, plus the fishy milk and the fennel juices to make a smooth white sauce, stirring all the time over gentle heat. Allow to simmer and thicken for 10 minutes, then taste and season.

Now for the assembly. Preheat the oven if it's not already on to Gas 4/350F/180C. Butter a baking dish, 12 × 8 × 2in/30 × 20 × 5cm (or 3 dishes for the larger quantity), and ladle a little sauce over the bottom. Lay about a third of the lasagne sheets over the bottom (I am assuming the no-pre-cook lasagne, or else you need to cook it first in lots of boiling salted water), cover with half the fish and fennel mixture, season with salt and pepper, ladle sauce on top, add another third of the lasagne sheets, the rest of the fish and fennel, season, ladle on more sauce, then add a final layer of lasagne. You should have enough sauce left for a generous top layer; if not, add some more milk to what remains, stir well over a gentle heat for a few minutes – a teaspoon or two of cornflour mixed into a tablespoon of cold milk and whisked into the sauce will help to thicken it. Pour the sauce over the top and sprinkle with grated cheese. Parmesan and Cheddar make a good mixture but any mature hard cheese will do.

Bake in the centre of the oven for 30–40 minutes, until the top is golden and bubbly.

Serve with crusty bread and a green salad. I fed 14 generously on twice the basic recipe.

Puddings

HOT CHOCOLATE SAUCE PUDDING 

This recipe came from Hilary Hanson at the Sheldon Retreat Centre as 'the most popular pudding in the clergy family holiday weeks' and may seem familiar – I have met it before as Debden Pudding, Denver Pudding and Chocolate Brownie Pudding. Whatever the name, it is a winner, emerging from the unlikely method in the recipe as a chocolate sponge in its own rich chocolate sauce.

For 6–8

For the sponge

6oz/175g self-raising flour
6oz/175g soft margarine
6oz/175g Fairtrade soft light brown sugar
3 Tbsp Fairtrade cocoa powder (unsweetened)
3 medium free-range eggs

For the topping/sauce

5 Tbsp Fairtrade demerara sugar
5 Tbsp Fairtrade cocoa powder

For 20

For the sponge

1lb 4oz/600g self-raising flour
1lb 4oz/600g soft margarine
1lb 4oz/600g Fairtrade soft light brown sugar
10 Tbsp Fairtrade cocoa powder (unsweetened)
10 medium free-range eggs

For the topping/sauce

15 Tbsp Fairtrade demerara sugar
15 Tbsp Fairtrade cocoa powder

1¼ pints/700ml boiling water	3¾ pints/2 litres boiling water

Preheat your oven to Gas 4/350F/180C.

Put all the sponge ingredients in a mixing bowl or processor and beat until thoroughly combined. Pour into a well-greased baking dish – it should come halfway up.

Sift the cocoa onto the demerara sugar and sprinkle all over the top of the pudding.

Pour the boiling water over it – yes, really! – and bake in the oven for 35–40 minutes until the sponge on top is set and the sauce has formed underneath.

Serve hot or warm, with creamy yogurt or pouring cream.

Note: The larger quantity will take longer to cook if it is in one extra large dish and you may need to turn the oven down or cover the top with paper to prevent scorching. Don't be tempted to use drinking chocolate instead of cocoa; the flavour will be insipid and the whole thing too sweet.

PEARS BAKED IN WINE ☺

This is the recipe to use for those hard green unripe pears, usually Conference, which are all too often on the supermarket shelves. The slow baking redeems them; at Christmas you might use some leftover spicy punch for the liquid, at other times try this combination.

First find a casserole or ovenproof pot (with a lid) which will just fit the number of pears you want to cook. The closer the fit, the less liquid needed to cover them. I use a tall earthenware pot and set the pears upright in it, putting the last few in upside down to fill in the gaps.

For every 1lb/450g of hard pears you will need:

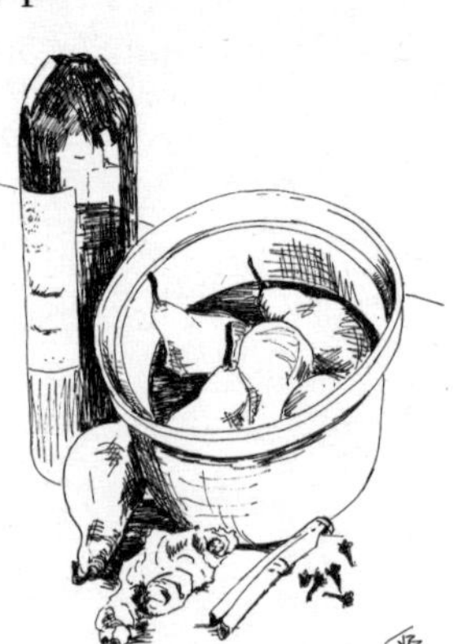

4–5oz/120–150g Fairtrade demerara sugar
1 cinnamon stick
1in/2cm piece of fresh root ginger
4 cloves
½ pint/280ml red wine

Preheat the oven to Gas 2/300F/150C.

Peel the pears whole, leaving the stalks on, and pack them closely into your chosen pot. Add the sugar and spices and then pour on the wine. Add enough water to cover the pears.

Cover the pot and bake in a slow oven until the pears are tender – anything from 1 to 4 hours.

Lift the pears out carefully and set them on a pretty dish. Boil down the juice in the casserole (or if your pot is earthenware, use a saucepan) until thick and syrupy and pour over the pears.

Serve hot or chilled with pouring cream.

CARAMEL ORANGES

Fruit puddings are much appreciated in the winter months and these oranges sit very well beside chocolate puddings on the dessert table. I give quantities for 12 – you can up- or downsize the recipe as long as you allow 1 orange per person. The thin-skinned navel oranges available in January and February are the best. The alcohol is optional, though good, and you can make it a day or two in advance.

For 12

12 navel oranges
2–3 Tbsp brandy or orange liqueur (optional)
½ pint/280ml water
8oz/225g granulated sugar

Peel the oranges with a sharp knife, making sure you remove all the pith. Cut across into slices. Arrange in layers in a heat-proof dish – a white soufflé dish is good – and sprinkle each layer with alcohol, if used.

Heat the sugar and water in a saucepan over moderate heat, stirring until the sugar has dissolved. Then boil rapidly, without stirring, until it turns a golden caramel colour. Keep an eye once it turns, so that it doesn't blacken too much. Pour immediately over the oranges and leave in the cool for an hour or two. The sheet of caramel will dissolve into a delicious syrup.

CHOCOLATE CRUNCH CHRISTMAS PUDDING

Here is a look-alike Christmas pudding for those who do not relish the real thing – it's a pudding-shaped version of chocolate biscuit cake and is very easy to make, with some melting to do but no real cooking. Put the biscuits in a sealed polythene bag and crush them with a rolling pin. The recipe is from Josceline Dimbleby's *Christmas Book* (Sainsbury 1987).

For 8–10

6oz/175g butter, plus more for greasing
3 Tbsp golden syrup
8oz/225g Fairtrade plain chocolate
6oz/175g ginger biscuits, crushed
6oz/175g plain sweet biscuits, crushed
1oz/25g Fairtrade currants or sultanas
3oz/75g Fairtrade raisins
2oz/50g glacé cherries, chopped roughly
1oz/25g ground cinnamon
2 Tbsp brandy or rum

For the icing

3oz Fairtrade plain chocolate
1 Tbsp water
1oz/25g butter
a little icing sugar
2–3 halved glacé cherries (optional)
a sprig of holly (optional)

Butter generously a 2 pint/1.2 litre pudding basin. Gently melt together the butter, syrup and chocolate in a large saucepan, stirring. Mix in the rest of the ingredients – biscuits, fruit, cinnamon and alcohol – and spoon it all into the pudding basin, pressing it well down.

Chill in the fridge; you could freeze it at this stage but it will keep perfectly well for a week or so. On the day, defrost if need be then dip the basin briefly in very hot water and turn the pudding out onto a serving dish.

For the icing, melt the chocolate in the water over a gentle heat and stir until smooth. Add the butter and stir until melted. Cool for a few minutes, then cover the pudding all over with the melted chocolate.

When cold, sprinkle with icing sugar for a snowy effect and if you like, place the cherries in a cluster on top and stick a sprig of holly in. Keep in a cool place but not the fridge. Serve in thin cake slices – it's very rich.

ELIZABETH RAFFALD'S ORANGE CUSTARDS

While Seville oranges are in the shops (one of the few fruits still properly seasonal), make these rich little custards as a party pudding. Elizabeth Raffald was an eighteenth-century cook and cookery writer. The number of servings depends on the size of your ramekins or custard cups.

For 8–10

1 Seville orange
1 Tbsp brandy or orange liqueur
4oz/100g Fairtrade granulated sugar
4 large egg yolks
½ pint/300ml double cream
½ pint/300ml single cream
candied orange peel in the piece (optional)

Preheat the oven to Gas 3/325F/170C.

Pare half the rind from the scrubbed orange with a potato peeler. Simmer it in water in a small pan for 2 minutes, drain and put in the liquidiser with the brandy or liqueur, juice of the orange, sugar and egg yolks. Blend at top speed until the peel is thoroughly blasted into tiny pieces.

Bring the creams to the boil in a pan and pour them gradually into the mixture in the blender, turning the blades at slow speed just to mix well. Check the seasoning and add more sugar or a little more orange juice if necessary.

Pour into 8–10 custard cups or small ramekins. Stand them in a roasting pan with hot water halfway up and place them in the oven until just set – about 30 minutes.

Garnish if you like with a sliver of candied orange peel cut from the piece in each ramekin. Serve either warm (nicest) or chilled.

ROLLED LEMON CREAM ☺

Another very quick and easy and deliciously rich pudding, which comes from our priest friend Graham. It takes only a few minutes to make and will last 3–4 days in the fridge. These quantities will make plenty for 8 people – it is very rich. You can easily make more – 1½ times for 12, and so on.

For 8–10

1 pint/570ml double cream
4 dessertspoons granulated sugar
juice of 1½ lemons

Pour the cream into a large saucepan and stir in the sugar. Bring to a rolling boil (so that it rises in the pan), remove from the heat before it boils over, add the lemon juice and leave to cool. Stir it again if need be – it should be really thick and smooth – and refrigerate.

Serve in small quantities, on its own or alongside soft fruit, maybe with sponge fingers or crisp almond biscuits.

CHESTNUT AND CHOCOLATE CAKE

This is a gluten-free recipe. It was sent by a friend who found it in a magazine and was a great success at our Shrove Tuesday party recently. I made it in advance and froze it. Make sure you buy *unsweetened* chestnut purée, as the recipe has quite a lot of other sugar and should not taste oversweet.

You need a clip-sided 8in/20cm cake tin at least 3in/8cm deep.

For 8

8oz/225g Fairtrade caster sugar
4 large eggs, separated
9oz/250g tin unsweetened chestnut purée
5oz/150g Fairtrade dark chocolate

Preheat the oven to Gas 4/350F/180C.

Butter the clip-sided cake tin well and line the base with non-stick silicone paper.

Put the sugar and egg yolks into a medium bowl and whisk them together until pale and fluffy (a Kenwood or small hand-held electric whisk is useful but you can do it with a rotary hand whisk). Fold in the chestnut purée, mixing thoroughly.

Melt the chocolate in a small bowl in the microwave or set over a pan of boiling water, and fold that into the egg yolk and chestnut mixture.

In a large bowl whisk the egg whites to stiff peaks. Fold two tablespoons of the white into the yolk mixture, then fold the mixture gradually into the whites and fold all together.

Pour into the cake tin and bake for 30–40 minutes. Cool before removing from the tin.

Serve with pouring cream, crème fraîche or Greek yogurt.

Note: If you have only one whisk, make sure it is thoroughly clean and dry before you use it a second time for the egg whites.

BLACKCURRANT PARFAIT

! 5–12 hours' freezing needed

Josceline Dimbleby's recipe for Orange Parfait (*Salads for All Seasons*, Sainsbury 1981) has become a regular on our party pudding table – in fact it is the only ice cream I make regularly – because it is light and delicious, easy to make and can be served straight from the freezer. Unfortunately, Sainsbury's seems to have stopped selling the little cylinders of frozen concentrated orange juice which were an essential part of the recipe, so now I make the parfaits with a strong blackcurrant extract, using fruit from our garden. You could use any really well-flavoured concentrated juice or fruit purée (you will need more of the purée). The quantities will serve 8–10 alongside other puddings.

You need a 4 pint/2.25 litre plastic bowl with lid and an electric beater.

For 8–10

3 large egg whites
a pinch of salt
8oz/225g Fairtrade granulated sugar
¼ pint/150ml water
¼ pint/150ml frozen blackcurrant extract (see page 218)
or ¾ pint/450ml fruit purée, unsweetened
½ pint/300ml whipping cream

Whisk the egg whites with the salt in the mixer bowl until they stand in soft peaks. Dissolve the sugar in the water in a small pan over low heat, then bring to the boil and boil fiercely for 3 minutes. Pour at once onto the egg whites, whisking at the highest speed as you pour. Whisk until it is thick and glossy, then whisk in the slightly thawed blackcurrant extract or fruit purée.

In another bowl whisk the cream until thick but not stiff and fold it into the purple mixture.

Pour into the plastic bowl, cover and freeze for at least 5 hours; better overnight.

Note: This becomes an all-year-round pudding if you keep fruit extract in the freezer (see page 218).

Spring

March, April, May

Lent with its leaner diet fits the 'hungry gap' time of year before the new crops of young vegetables appear to delight our taste buds – new potatoes, broad beans, young carrots and turnips to go with Easter lamb. Enjoy the last of the citrus fruits, early rhubarb and watch for the first gooseberries (traditionally for Whitsun).

Spring

Soups and Starters

Fennel Soup with Ginger and Garlic
Carrot and Basil Soup
Green Pea Soup
Atlas Mountain Soup
Locket's Savoury
Potted Lentils with Mushroom
Hummus
Blinis

Main Courses

Greek Easter Lamb
Chilli con Carne Extra
Chicken Firuzabad with Fluffy Rice
Spring Lamb Fillets with Sesame and Coriander
V Black-eyed Beanfeast
V Lucy's Lentil Gratin
V Oven-baked Mushroom and Chestnut Risotto
V Couscous Salad with Roasted Vegetables and Feta Cheese
Peasant-style Fish and Potato Stew
Rich Man Poor Man Lunch

Puddings

Rhubarb and Orange Compôte
Rhubarb Stirabout
Orange Halva Cake
St Clement's Trifle
Pineapple and Ginger Salad
Molten Chocolate Moulds
Seville Chocolate Mousse

Soups and Starters

FENNEL SOUP WITH GINGER AND GARLIC

In the old days, nettle soup was recommended to cleanse the system in the spring. This fennel soup, with fresh ginger and garlic to stimulate us, is perhaps a modern equivalent. It comes from Rosamond Richardson's *Complete Vegetarian Cooking* (Sainsbury 1991).

For 6–8	*For 20*
2 Tbsp sesame or sunflower oil	3 Tbsp sesame or sunflower oil
9 fat cloves garlic, peeled and sliced	20 fat cloves garlic, peeled and sliced
3 medium heads fennel, chopped	8 medium heads fennel, chopped
1½oz/35g root ginger, peeled and finely chopped	3oz/80g root ginger, peeled and finely chopped
3 pints/1.8 litres vegetable stock	8 pints/4.8 litres vegetable stock
soy sauce to taste	soy sauce to taste

Heat the oil in a large saucepan, add the garlic and cook gently for 4–5 minutes, stirring to make sure it softens without burning. Add the chopped fennel and stir for about 10 minutes until it begins to soften. Add the chopped ginger and the stock and bring to a gentle simmer. Cover and cook for about 25 minutes. Remove from the heat.

Liquidise, in batches if need be, return to the pan and season with soy sauce.

CARROT AND BASIL SOUP

Carrots are often partnered with parsley but I learned from Gina, an old peasant friend in Italy, to serve them with shredded basil leaves. Here is a carrot and basil soup which makes a cheerful start to a spring meal.

For 6–8	*For 20*
2oz/50g butter	6oz/175g butter
1½lb/700g carrots, chopped	5lb/2.4kg carrots, chopped
1 large onion, chopped	3 onions, chopped
1 large potato, peeled and chopped	3 potatoes, peeled and chopped
1 stick celery, chopped	3 sticks celery, chopped
2½ pints/1.5 litres vegetable stock	7 pints/4 litres vegetable stock
½ pint/280ml milk	1½ pints/850ml milk
3 sprigs of basil	6–8 sprigs of basil
salt and pepper	salt and pepper
3 Tbsp single cream (optional)	½ pint/280ml single cream (optional)

Heat the butter in a large pan and sweat the vegetables gently in it, turning them to absorb the butter. After 5–10 minutes, add the stock and most of the basil – keep a few leaves for garnish but add all the stalks. Cover and simmer till all the vegetables are cooked.

Liquidise, in batches if need be. Season to taste. Serve with the cream stirred in, if used, and a sprinkle of torn basil leaves.

GREEN PEA SOUP

Split peas make a good autumn or winter soup (see page 10) but by spring we are looking for lighter, fresher tasting soups and this one, even though it uses frozen peas, gives us a foretaste of summer. Leeks marry well with the smoothness of the peas and the potatoes make an easy thickening.

For 6–8	*For 20*
3oz/80g butter	6oz/175g butter
2 onions, chopped	5 onions, chopped
3 leeks, cleaned and sliced finely	8 leeks, cleaned and sliced finely
1lb/450g frozen peas	3lb/1.35kg frozen peas
3 pints/1.8 litres vegetable stock	8 pints/5 litres vegetable stock
12oz/350g potatoes, peeled and chopped	2lb/900g potatoes, peeled and chopped
salt and pepper	salt and pepper
¼ pint/150ml single cream	¾ pint/425ml single cream
a little chopped mint	2 Tbsp chopped mint

Heat the butter in a large saucepan, add the onions and leeks, turn well in the butter, cover and soften for 5–10 minutes. Add the peas and stir them in the butter too. Then add the warmed stock and the potato pieces and season to taste with salt and pepper. Bring to the boil, cover and simmer till the vegetables are soft – about 30 minutes.

Liquidise the soup, in batches if need be, return to the pan, stir in the cream and reheat. Sprinkle with a little chopped mint and serve.

This is also good chilled, in which case chill the creamed soup and add the mint as you serve it.

ATLAS MOUNTAIN SOUP

! apricots need 2 hours' soaking

This is the soup I have made most often, whenever we have needed a meal in a bowl. Its genius lies in the tangy combination of lemon and apricot with the spiced vegetable and meat stew. It is universally enjoyed and is simple to make, though quite a lot of chopping is involved if you are making the larger quantity. Make sure you have enough large bowls for serving – it is not a mug soup. This recipe comes from Josceline Dimbleby's *Marvellous Meals with Mince* (Sainsbury 1982).

For 6–8	*For 20*
6oz/175g Fairtrade dried apricots	1lb/450g Fairtrade dried apricots
3 Tbsp olive oil	4 Tbsp olive oil
3 cloves garlic, chopped finely	4–5 cloves garlic, chopped finely
3 tsp ground cinnamon	2 Tbsp ground cinnamon
3 tsp ground cumin	2 Tbsp ground cumin
3 tsp paprika	2 Tbsp paprika
1½lb/700g minced lamb or beef	4lb/1.8kg minced lamb or beef
6 sticks celery, cut in 1–2in/2.5–5cm pieces	12 sticks celery, cut in 1–2in/2.5–5cm pieces
1½ large green peppers, sliced	3 large green peppers, sliced
1½lb/700g tomatoes, sliced roughly	4lb/1.8kg tomatoes, sliced roughly
1 large lemon	3 large lemons
1 pint/600ml water	2½ pints/1.5 litres water
1 Tbsp Fairtrade demerara sugar	2 Tbsp Fairtrade demerara sugar
salt and black pepper	salt and black pepper

Soak the apricots in water for at least 2 hours or more, then drain.

Heat the oil in a large, heavy saucepan over moderate heat. Add the garlic and spices and stir for a minute. Add the mince, turn up the heat and stir briskly, breaking up the mince and browning it all over. Add the drained apricots and the celery, green pepper and tomato.

Shave 10–12 strips of peel from the lemon (20–25 for the larger recipe) and add to the soup with the lemon juice. Stir in the water and then season with the sugar, salt and pepper.

Taste and adjust seasoning. Bring to the boil, cover and simmer for 30 minutes. Serve with plenty of crusty bread.

This soup can be made in advance and reheated, but don't let it cook any longer.

LOCKET'S SAVOURY

I give this recipe (originally from Locket's restaurant in London) because it is so delicious, though rather messy to eat and probably too extravagant with the cheese to be useful for large numbers.

For 6–8

6 slices of white bread
1–2 bunches of watercress
4 large ripe aromatic pears, peeled and sliced
12oz Stilton cheese, sliced
black pepper to grind

Preheat the oven to Gas 4/350F/180C.

Toast the bread on one side only, cut each slice in half and lay soft side up on a baking tray. Spread the watercress over the top, as evenly as possible, and then the slices of peeled pears. Cover with the slices of Stilton cheese and put in the oven for about 10 minutes until the cheese begins to melt. Grind the black pepper over and serve.

POTTED LENTILS WITH MUSHROOM

Two simple vegetarian pâtés next, very economical and a good contrast in colours – this lentil recipe comes out intriguingly black and the hummus a pleasant sandy colour.

This recipe is from Gail Ballinger – as she says, it is good for Lent lunches. The quantities are enough for 15–20 alongside other dips and pâtés.

Makes 6–8 small ramekins

8oz/225g split red lentils
¾ pint/400ml water
3½oz/100g butter
8oz/225g well-flavoured mushrooms, chopped fine
1 large clove garlic, chopped fine
2 Tbsp chopped parsley
lemon juice to taste
salt and pepper

Cook the lentils in the water until they are soft and have absorbed it all – about 30–40 minutes, depending on the age of the lentils.

Melt the butter in a frying pan and sauté the mushrooms with the garlic over a light heat for 3–4 minutes, lifting and turning all the time. Stir in the parsley. Combine the lentils and mushroom mixture in a blender, seasoned well with salt and pepper and as much lemon juice as you want, and whiz to a soft purée.

Turn out into small dishes, cover and chill.

Note: You can give this a bit of zip when serving by sprinkling a very little cayenne pepper over each ramekin and trailing a little olive oil over the cayenne. Serve with crackers, toast or oatcakes.

HUMMUS

! overnight soaking needed

Hummus, however you spell it, is a wonderful pâté to serve: tasty, nourishing, cheap and vegetarian. Remember to start the night before by soaking the chickpeas. My recipe is based on one by Lionel Blue, and is enough for 15–20 alongside other dips and pâtés.

8oz/225g chickpeas, soaked overnight in plenty of water
2 whole cloves garlic, peeled
2 pinches of cayenne pepper
2 tsp cumin seeds, crushed
salt and pepper
juice of 1–2 lemons
1–2 Tbsp tahini paste
4–6 Tbsp olive oil

Soak the chickpeas overnight. Bring them to the boil in the same water in a large pan with the garlic, cayenne, cumin seeds and a grind or two of black pepper. Simmer, covered, until tender, for about 2–2½ hours. Add salt after the peas are cooked.

Liquidise the peas with enough spiced water to blend easily in batches. As you go, add the lemon juice, olive oil and tahini paste and taste from time to time, adjusting the seasoning if need be.

To serve, spread on a wide dish, make patterns with a fork and trickle olive oil into them and sprinkle a pinch or two of cayenne pepper over the top.

Serve with toast or crusty bread.

BLINIS

These have become our Shrove Tuesday pancakes in recent years, providing a delicious first course, laid out on a table where guests help themselves to blinis, sour cream or crème fraîche and a topping of caviar, smoked salmon, anchovy or prosciutto. They are small, about 2in/5cm in diameter.

This version uses half buckwheat, half plain flour; if you like the rather strong flavour, you can increase the proportion of buckwheat, or use all buckwheat, making them gluten-free (buckwheat is not wheat at all but a member of the dock family).

Makes 40–50 blinis

4oz/110g buckwheat flour } or 8oz/220g buckwheat flour
4oz/110g strong white flour }
1 tsp black pepper, freshly ground
1½ tsp salt
½oz/15g fresh yeast
¾ pint/420ml warm milk
2 eggs, separated

Mix the flours, pepper and salt in a large bowl.

Put the yeast in a small bowl and stir in a little of the warm water to make a cream. Gradually add the rest of the milk, stirring.

Make a well in the middle of the flour mixture, put in the egg yolks and stir in the milk mixture to make a smooth batter. Cover the bowl with oiled clingfilm and leave in a warm place for about an hour. It will begin to ferment and bubble.

Whisk the egg whites with a pinch of salt until stiff but not dry and fold them into the bubbly batter. Cover again with the clingfilm and leave to ferment for about an hour.

Brush a large heavy frying pan lightly with oil and place over moderate heat. Using a tablespoon of batter at a time, ladle it into the frying pan to make small rounds. Tiny holes will appear on the surface. Turn them with a palette knife to cook on the other side, then stack them on a clean cloth. Keep warm while you cook the rest of the blinis.

You can keep the batter overnight in the fridge if more convenient, removing it an hour before you need to make them. Blinis reheat well in a moderate oven, stacked and covered with foil.

Note: Shrove Tuesday is only a suggestion – blinis are welcome at any time of the year.

Main Courses

GREEK EASTER LAMB

The Greek Orthodox recipe we use for our Easter lamb is full of Passover symbolism: the sacrificial lamb, the bitter herbs and the cooking of it all in one dish to remind us of the last Passover meal. It is happy to sit in a low oven till you are ready for it and is very delicious.

For 8–10

5–6lb/2–2.5kg joint of lamb (see below)
rosemary and garlic
salt and pepper
olive oil
2–3lb/900g–1.3kg potatoes
2lb/900g tomatoes

Buy a whole shoulder of lamb, or a leg and half a shoulder or, if you live in lamb country and can get it, half a very young lamb, shoulder and leg together. This is often possible in Italy or France but seldom in England.

Preheat the oven to Gas 7/425F/220C. Make deep cuts in the meat and push slivers of garlic into them with small sprigs of rosemary. Season well with salt and pepper. Put a little olive oil in your largest roasting pan, put in the meat and start it roasting while you prepare the potatoes.

Scrub the potatoes, slice them thickly and bring just to the boil in salted water. Drain well, then place all around the meat, turning them in the oil. Once the meat has started to colour, turn the oven down to Gas 4/350F/180C.

Now cut up the tomatoes roughly and lay them over the potatoes. Grind black pepper over them and leave it all to cook together for about 1½–2 hours. You can turn the oven down another notch and leave it for longer; use the bottom oven in an Aga.

Depending on the size of your pan and your party, you may need to roast some more potatoes separately; if so use olive oil for best taste and texture. No gravy with this recipe but the meat will be tender and juicy and the vegetables moist with tomato and meat juice. Serve with the seasonal vegetables – maybe new little turnips and a few carrots and some late purple sprouting broccoli.

CHILLI CON CARNE EXTRA

! overnight soaking needed if dried beans used

Josceline Dimbleby's version of this classic dish is our favourite; she uses dark chocolate in Mexican fashion to add depth and sweetness to the spicy flavour and fresh chillies to give it real zip. Don't be afraid of serving well-spiced dishes, particularly if there is something else to choose for the unadventurous.

For 6–8	*For 20*
10oz/275g dried or 2 × 14oz/400g tins red kidney beans	1¼lb/600g dried or 5 × 14oz/400g tins red kidney beans
3 Tbsp olive oil	5 Tbsp olive oil
3 medium onions, sliced	5 medium onions, sliced
1½lb/700g minced beef	3½lb/1.6kg minced beef
3 tsp ground cinnamon	5 tsp ground cinnamon
1–3 small fresh chillies, green or red	3–5 small fresh chillies, green or red
1½ × 14oz/400g tins tomatoes, chopped	3 × 14oz/400g tins tomatoes, chopped
1½oz/35g Fairtrade plain chocolate	3oz/80g Fairtrade plain chocolate
3 Tbsp water	6 Tbsp water
salt	salt
plenty of chopped parsley	plenty of chopped parsley

If using dried beans, soak in water for 8 hours or overnight. Then boil them in unsalted fresh water for 1 hour, boiling rapidly for at least 10 minutes first to destroy toxins, and drain.

Heat the oil in a large heavy pan and stir in the onions over a medium heat until soft. Increase the heat, add the beef and dig around for a few minutes until brown. Lower the heat again and add the cinnamon.

Cut open the chillies under running water and remove the seeds; then chop them finely. Add them to the pan together with the drained, cooked beans and the tomatoes. In a small saucepan, melt the chocolate in the water gently and stir into the bean and meat mixture. Season well with salt.

Cover and simmer for 1 hour. Check seasoning. Stir in the parsley before serving. Crusty bread and a green salad go well with this.

Note: For a vegetarian alternative, see the recipe for Lentil Moussaka (see pages 26–7).

CHICKEN FIRUZABAD WITH FLUFFY RICE

! the rice needs an hour's soaking

This exotic chicken dish is convenient in that the rice and chicken finish cooking together in the same casserole. For the same reason, it is probably a dish to make for 12 rather than 20, though if you have enough large casseroles you could make more. We like thigh, drumstick and wing joints as well as breast, so if you can buy a mixture, so much the better. Thanks to Josceline Dimbleby for this one.

For 10–12

1½lb/700g Fairtrade basmati rice
4 Tbsp sea salt
4oz/120g butter
2 Tbsp olive oil
3 large onions, chopped
12–14 free-range chicken joints, mixed (see above)
8oz/225g Fairtrade dried apricots, halved
6oz/175g Fairtrade pitted prunes, halved
6oz/175g almonds in their skins
2 tsp cinnamon
3 pints/1.7 litres water
salt and pepper

At least an hour before you start cooking the chicken, rinse the rice thoroughly in a sieve. Put it in a bowl, add the salt, cover with warm water and leave to soak.

Take a large flameproof casserole (you'll need a bigger one later) and in it melt half the butter with the oil over a medium heat. Add the onion, stir and cook for a few minutes until soft. Using a slotted spoon, remove the onion to a plate on one side. Turn up the heat and fry the chicken joints all over, in batches, to brown well. Then return the onions and all the chicken to the pan together with the apricots, prunes and almonds. Sprinkle on the cinnamon and season with salt and pepper. Pour in the water. Bring to the boil, cover and simmer gently for 30–40 minutes, until the chicken is tender.

Meanwhile bring a large pan of salted water to the boil, drain the soaked rice and add it to the boiling water for 4–6 minutes; it should remain underdone. Drain, rinse and leave on one side.

When the chicken is cooked, lift out the joints and keep them on one side. Boil up the juices and fruit in the casserole, uncovered, until the sauce has reduced to a syrup. Take your largest casserole, melt the rest of the butter in it, put in the drained rice and arrange the chicken joints on top, spooning the syrupy sauce over them. Cover with a tea towel and then the lid and put in the lowest part of the oven for 20–25 minutes. The rice will be fluffy and tender.

Serve with a green salad.

SPRING LAMB FILLETS WITH SESAME AND CORIANDER ☺

! marinate for several hours

This is the most delicious and convenient recipe I know for a spring or early summer dinner party – sit-down food rather than a stand-up affair. The fillets are marinated beforehand and only need 15–20 minutes in the oven, so they can go in just as you sit down to a first course. New young vegetables go very well: new potatoes, whole young carrots, mange-tout peas or young spinach. It is another of Josceline Dimbleby's recipes, from *Festive Food and Party Pieces* (Sainsbury 1982). I find that 4 fillets feed 6 people.

For 10–12

4 Tbsp sesame or sunflower oil
juice of 2 lemons
4 good Tbsp sesame seeds
2 Tbsp coriander seeds, crushed finely
4–5 cloves garlic, crushed
4–5 pinches cayenne pepper
6–8 lamb neck fillets (about 6–8oz/160–225g each)
salt
lettuce leaves or large mint leaves,
chopped coriander to serve

Mix the oil, lemon juice, the seeds, garlic and cayenne together. Rub this mixture onto the fillets and lay them in a shallow roasting pan (not an old metal one which the lemon might corrode; choose a stainless steel or fireproof or pottery one or else line it with foil). Cover loosely with foil and leave in a cool place to marinate, turning the fillets once or twice, for several hours or overnight.

To cook, heat the oven to Gas 9/475F/240C, remove the foil cover and cook at the very top of the oven for 15–20 minutes, no more. Remove and allow to rest for a few minutes, to distribute the pinkness through the meat, which will be tender and juicy.

Carve the fillets crossways into thin slices with a sharp knife. Lay the slices, overlapping, on a warm flat serving dish decorated with the lettuce or mint leaves. Sprinkle the meat with a little salt and the coriander and pour the pan juices over it.

BLACK-EYED BEANFEAST

! overnight soaking needed

Another bean dish, this time using black-eyed beans, which is fit for a party and good hot or cold. It comes from a Sainsbury cookbook, *The Vegetarian Gourmet*, by Rosamond Richardson (1985).

For 6–8	*For 20*
12oz/350g black-eyed beans, soaked overnight	1½lb/700g black-eyed beans, soaked overnight
4 Tbsp vegetable oil	8 Tbsp vegetable oil
1½ tsp cumin seeds	3 tsp cumin seeds
1 tsp cinnamon powder	2 tsp cinnamon powder
12oz/350g onions, chopped	1½lb/700g onions, chopped
4 cloves garlic, sliced	6 cloves garlic, sliced
20oz/700g tinned tomatoes, chopped	3 × 14oz/400g tins tomatoes, chopped
12oz/350g mushrooms, sliced	1½lb/700g mushrooms, sliced
3 tsp coriander seeds	2 Tbsp coriander seeds
1 tsp each of ground cumin, turmeric and cayenne pepper	2 tsp each of ground cumin, turmeric and cayenne pepper
4 Tbsp chopped parsley	8 Tbsp chopped parsley
salt and freshly ground pepper	salt and freshly ground pepper

Drain the soaked beans and boil in a saucepan with 2 pints/1.2 litres of fresh water (4+ pints/2.3+ litres for the larger quantity). Bring to the boil and boil rapidly for 10 minutes.

Meanwhile, heat the oil in a large pan and sizzle the cumin seeds and cinnamon in it for a few seconds. Add the onions and garlic and stir for a minute or two. Add the tomatoes, mushrooms and remaining spices and parsley. Simmer for 10 minutes.

Add the beans with enough of their liquid to just cover the mixture, put on the lid and simmer for 30 minutes.

Taste, add salt and pepper as necessary and allow to stand a while before serving.

Note: If you are serving cold, keep the parsley to stir into it when cool.

LUCY'S LENTIL GRATIN

Our lute-playing friend Lucy brought a dish of these lentils to a music weekend: we have made it ever since. It is one of those vegetarian dishes which everyone makes for, herbi- and carnivore alike. What makes it special is the cream and walnut and Gruyère topping. But it is not an extravagant recipe and you can use Emmenthal or Jarlsberg or a mixture if Gruyère is beyond your budget. It is very filling; I have given as the larger amount what fills my biggest ovenproof dish (5 pints/3 litres), which will feed at least 12 as a main course and 15–20 as an 'extra' for tempted carnivores. The recipe came originally from a packet of Le Puy lentils.

For 6–8	*For 12–20 (see above)*
10oz/300g Le Puy lentils	1lb 2oz/500g Le Puy lentils
2 medium carrots, grated	1lb 2oz/500g medium carrots, grated
1 leek, chopped	9oz/250g leeks, chopped
2 medium onions, chopped	9oz/250g medium onions, chopped
1oz/25g butter	2oz/50g butter
¼ pint/150ml cream	½ pint/300ml cream
6–8oz/175–225g Gruyère, grated	12oz–1lb/350–500g Gruyère, grated
salt and pepper	salt and pepper
1oz/25g Fairtrade walnuts	2oz/50g Fairtrade walnuts

Preheat the oven to Gas 4/350F/180C.

Cook the lentils gently in water till tender – about 30–40 minutes.

Meanwhile, prepare the vegetables. Melt the butter in a large pan and cook the carrots, leek and onions very gently, so they sweat rather than brown.

Add the cooked lentils, 2 Tbsp cream (4 Tbsp for the larger

amount) and half the cheese, mix well, season with salt and pepper. Transfer into a shallow ovenproof dish. Chop or process the walnuts and mix with the rest of the cream and cheese. Spread on top of the lentil mixture.

Bake for 20 minutes, till golden and bubbling.

OVEN-BAKED MUSHROOM AND CHESTNUT RISOTTO

! overnight soaking needed if dried chestnuts used

This is a well-flavoured and good-natured dish which will keep warm happily till it is needed and adapt well for large numbers. Thanks to Gail Ballinger for this one.

For 6–8	*For 20*
4oz/100g dried chestnuts, soaked overnight *or* 8oz/200g vacuum pack of cooked chestnuts	8oz/225g dried chestnuts, soaked overnight *or* 2 × 8oz/200g vacuum pack of cooked chestnuts
1½ pints/900ml hot vegetable stock	3 pints/1.8 litres hot vegetable stock
3oz/75g butter *or* 3 Tbsp olive oil	5oz/175g butter *or* 5 Tbsp olive oil
1 large onion, chopped	2 large onions, chopped
12oz/350g chestnut mushrooms, quartered	2lb/900g chestnut mushrooms, quartered
12oz/350g risotto rice	2lb/900g risotto rice
sprigs of thyme	sprigs of thyme
salt and pepper	salt and pepper

Unless you are using the ready-cooked chestnuts, first, cook the soaked chestnuts in some of the stock for about 20–30 minutes, till tender. Preheat the oven to Gas 2/300F/150C.

Melt the butter or heat the oil in an ovenproof casserole and soften the onions in it with the quartered mushrooms (cut them smaller if they are huge). Add the rice and stir until it has absorbed the fat – this will take longer with the larger quantity.

Add the chestnuts and the hot stock and thyme and bring it all to the boil. Put the casserole uncovered into the oven and cook for 30–35 minutes, keeping an eye in case it needs a little more stock. The rice should be tender but not mushy and all the stock absorbed. Taste, season and serve.

Note: If you can't get well-flavoured mushrooms, use ordinary ones but add a few pieces of dried boletus (ceps), soaked first.

COUSCOUS SALAD WITH ROASTED VEGETABLES AND FETA CHEESE

Mediterranean vegetables lend themselves to roasting – the flavour is intense and delicious. Folded into a couscous salad with a spicy dressing and feta cheese for protein, they make an excellent vegetarian dish. It is based on a Delia Smith recipe.

For 6–8	*For 20*
Vegetables	*Vegetables*
1 aubergine, cubed	3 aubergines, cubed
2 medium courgettes, sliced thinly	6 courgettes, cubed
2 red or yellow peppers, each cut into 8	6 red or yellow peppers, each cut into 8
2 onions, peeled and quartered	6 onions, peeled and quartered
1lb/450g tomatoes, quartered	2lb/1kg tomatoes, quartered
3 cloves garlic, quartered	9 cloves garlic, quartered
3 Tbsp olive oil	6 Tbsp olive oil
salt and pepper	salt and pepper
Couscous	*Couscous*
12oz/350g medium couscous	2lb/1kg medium couscous
1 pint/600ml vegetable stock stock	2¾ pints/1.6 litres vegetable
salt and pepper	salt and pepper
Dressing	*Dressing*
4fl oz/100ml olive oil	8fl oz/225ml olive oil
4 Tbsp lime (or lemon) juice	8 Tbsp lime (or lemon) juice
2 Tbsp ground cumin	4 Tbsp ground cumin
1 tsp cayenne pepper	2½ tsp cayenne pepper
2 Tbsp tomato purée	4 Tbsp tomato purée

To serve

4oz/110g feta cheese, cubed
flat leaf parsley, chopped

To serve

10oz/275kg feta cheese, cubed
flat leaf parsley, chopped

Preheat the oven to its highest: Gas 9/475F/240C.

Lay the prepared vegetables in a large roasting tin (or two, for the larger quantity); spoon on the oil and turn the vegetables in it to coat each piece. Season with salt and pepper and roast on the highest shelf for 30–40 minutes, until well cooked and charred at the edges.

Meanwhile, put the couscous in a large bowl, bring the stock to the boil and pour it over the couscous. Season with salt and pepper and stir with a fork, then leave to swell and absorb the liquid.

Put all the dressing ingredients in a jar and shake well.

To serve, mix the dressing into the couscous, then stir in the roasted vegetables and any juices from the pan. Finally add the cubed feta cheese and the chopped parsley.

PEASANT-STYLE FISH AND POTATO STEW

With many species of fish endangered through over-fishing it can be hard to know what to buy at the fish stall. Good fishmongers label the provenance of their fish; use that information, keep up to date as far as you can with the world scene and buy accordingly.

Fish will not normally be a sensible choice for feeding crowds of people – it doesn't like hanging around, nor does it reheat well, and it doesn't come cheap. But there are exceptions to that: a cold salmon in the summer can feed many people very well, a good fish pie can be made the day before and baked when you need it, and the Fish Goulash (see page 159) can be prepared in advance and the fish added for the last 20 minutes.

This fish and potato stew won't reheat well but can provide a good meal in a bowl without too much trouble.

For 6–8	*For 20*
2lb/900g white fish fillet (cod or other firm fish)	5–6lb/2.3–2.7kg white fish fillet (cod or other firm fish)
3 Tbsp olive oil	5 Tbsp olive oil
1–2 large red onions, sliced	3–4 large red onions, sliced
3 sticks celery, sliced	5 sticks celery, sliced
6 ripe tomatoes, chopped	10 ripe tomatoes, chopped
3 garlic cloves, chopped	5 garlic cloves, chopped
2 pints/1.2 litres fish stock (see page 216)	5–6 pints/3.5 litres fish stock (see page 216)
¼–½ pint/150–280ml dry white wine	½–1 pint/280–570ml dry white wine
2lb/900g new potatoes, scrubbed and quartered	5lb/2.3kg new potatoes, scrubbed and quartered
salt and black pepper	salt and black pepper
3 bay leaves	5 bay leaves
flat leaf parsley, chopped	flat leaf parsley, chopped

Cut the fish into 1in/2.5cm pieces and sprinkle with salt. Heat the oil in a flameproof casserole, add the onion and celery and soften over a gentle heat. Add the tomatoes, garlic, stock, wine, potatoes and seasoning. Bring to the boil and simmer for 10–15 minutes, till the potatoes are soft. Check the seasoning.

Add the fish and simmer till it is just cooked – 3–5 minutes.

Serve sprinkled with parsley, preferably flat leaf, in large warmed bowls with crusty French bread.

RICH MAN POOR MAN LUNCH

For Christian Aid Week or One World Week

This is a vivid way to help us become aware of the injustice in the world, of how whether you get enough to eat depends on where you were born, not on what you deserve. It points up the problem and leaves you to work out solutions.

You need:

1 A large room or hall, big enough to take 60 people.
2 60 people brave enough to take part.
3 Willing cooks to provide and serve a four-course feast for 4–5 people.
4 Willing cooks to provide and serve a simple ploughman's lunch for 12 people.
5 A willing cook to provide plain ungarnished boiled rice for others.

Here is how it works. You clear the room of tables except for two. One is in the centre of the room and laid for the feast for 4–5: candles, napkins, silver, etc. Put the other table against a wall with 12 plates of ploughman's set on it with a few chairs nearby.

When people come in, they all pay an agreed sum – maybe £5 – and draw a folded ticket from a container, as for a raffle draw. When they look at their ticket, it will be marked F for feast, P for ploughman's, or be blank.

The lucky Fs go to sit at the centre table. The Ps go to collect their plate of food. Everyone else mills around until a large pan of boiled rice appears (in the hatchway to the kitchen if there is one) and they queue for a bowl of plain rice, which they eat with their fingers, standing or squatting on the floor.

That's it. The interesting part is to see how they all react; how does it feel to be a 'lucky' one when you are set in the midst of the hungry? How do the hungry feel when they see others eating but are not included? Do the groups interact?

It is best not to spell out beforehand what is going to happen so that you get a more genuine response. If you want to follow up with informed discussion you can get help and information from Christian Aid (www.christianaid.org.uk).

If you are fortunate enough to have people from the third world in your community, you might get one of them to cook the rice authentically. I vividly remember Vietnamese mushy rice served at such a lunch in Portsmouth many years ago.

Puddings

RHUBARB AND ORANGE COMPÔTE

! needs to stand overnight and to cool after baking

When it first appears in the shops in early spring, whether pink and forced from Yorkshire or ruby red from Hampshire, rhubarb is a great treat. Try it combined with orange which seems to cut its acidity and set off its colour beautifully. This can be made a day or two beforehand.

For 10–12

5–6lb/2.25–2.7kg young rhubarb
5–6 large navel oranges
8–12oz/225–350g Fairtrade demerara sugar, to taste

Cut the rhubarb into 1in/2.5cm chunks. Remove the peel and pith from the oranges with a sharp knife, keeping the fruit whole. Slice them across the rounds.

Put layers of rhubarb alternately with layers of orange slices into a deep ovenproof pot or casserole with a lid, adding sugar as you go.

Allow to stand overnight if possible, to start the juices flowing. Next day, bake in a low to moderate oven, Gas 3–4/325–350F/170–180C, for about an hour, until the fruit is tender.

Cool, pour into a pretty bowl (pink if possible) and chill before serving.

Note: 6lb/2.7kg of rhubarb seems a lot but it does 'cook down'.

RHUBARB STIRABOUT ☺

Another favourite rhubarb recipe, this time for eating hot, perhaps at a large family Sunday lunch. It is quick to make, cooks while you are eating the main course and is very popular with children, especially if you let them spoon their own syrup. Another Hampshire recipe.

For 10–12

12oz/350g self-raising flour
6oz/175g butter or margarine
3 eggs
7fl oz/200ml milk
1½lb/700g rhubarb, cut in 1in/2.5cm pieces
6oz/170g Fairtrade granulated sugar
golden syrup to serve

Preheat the oven to Gas 7/425F/220C.

Rub the fat into the flour till it's like breadcrumbs. Add the eggs, beaten together with the milk. Stir in the rhubarb and the sugar.

Put it all into a well-greased large pie dish or 2 smaller ones, and bake in a hot oven for 30–40 minutes.

Serve hot, passing the jar of golden syrup around the company. No need for cream.

Note: The pudding itself is not very sweet, so the syrup is vital; honey would be a possible substitute.

ORANGE HALVA CAKE

Another Greek recipe to complete the Easter feast, though this halva cake is worth cooking for a party at any time. Best made the day before to give the syrup time to soak in.

For 8–10 at least

8oz/225g butter
8oz/225g Fairtrade granulated sugar
grated rind and juice of 2 small oranges
4 eggs
12oz/350g semolina
6oz/175g ground almonds
3 tsp baking powder
whipped cream and blanched almonds for decoration (optional)

For the syrup
6oz/175g Fairtrade granulated sugar
5 Tbsp water
2 Tbsp lemon juice
1 Tbsp candied peel
powdered cinnamon to taste
3 Tbsp orange juice

Preheat the oven to Gas 7/425F/220C. Butter a 9in/23cm ring mould. Cream the butter and sugar and grated orange rind together and mix in the juice. Whip the eggs in a bowl and add gradually to the butter mixture. Stir in the semolina, almonds and baking powder.

Turn into the ring mould (if you haven't one, use a spring-form cake tin) and bake in the hot oven for 10 minutes, then turn the heat down to Gas 4/350F/180C for 30 minutes more.

Meanwhile make the syrup. Boil together all the ingredients except the orange juice, uncovered in a small pan until slightly thickened, then remove from the heat and stir in the orange juice.

Turn the cake out of the mould as soon as possible after it is cooked and pour the syrup over slowly.

Serve cold. I usually fill the centre with whipped cream and stud the cake with halved blanched almonds.

ST CLEMENT'S TRIFLE ☺

! needs chilling for 4 hours

This version of a London club favourite, Boodles Fool, comes from my friend Louise, who is constantly entertaining large numbers. It has a lovely tangy taste and is not too sweet.

For 8–10

1 packet of trifle sponges
3 large oranges
2 small lemons
½ pint/280ml double cream
¼ pint/150ml single cream
2 Tbsp Fairtrade caster sugar

Cut each trifle sponge into 6 small squares. Place them in the bottom of a deep glass bowl. Grate the rind from the oranges and lemons and squeeze the juice. Whip the creams together till thick, preferably with an electric whisk.

Pour the juices gradually into the cream, continuing to whisk, and add the rind and sugar. Keep whisking until the cream thickens again. It will take a little time.

Pour the thickened mixture over the sponge pieces. Cover the bowl and chill for at least 4 hours, preferably overnight.

PINEAPPLE AND GINGER SALAD

Alongside the rich chocolate and creamy puddings we love to enjoy at parties, it is good to offer a sharper tasting fruity one. Pineapples, sometimes available with a Fairtrade label, are welcome at this time of year and this salad, flavoured with ginger and orange, is easy and popular. It can be made a day or two beforehand.

For 8–10

1 very large Fairtrade pineapple or 2 medium
6oz/150g Fairtrade granulated sugar
½ pint/300ml water
1 large orange or 2 small
1in/2.5cm piece of fresh root ginger, bruised
2 knobs ginger preserved in syrup from a jar

First peel and cut up your pineapple; stand it on a board and with a sharp knife cut the skin downwards after slicing off the plume. Remove any dark knots or bruised patches. Quarter the pineapple, slice out the hard core and cut up the rest into bite-sized pieces. Place them in a pretty bowl.

Now put the sugar and water in a small pan, stir over a gentle heat to melt the sugar, then bring to the boil. Add 4 or 5 strips of peel pared from the orange, the bruised ginger root and boil for 4–5 minutes. Remove from the heat, leave the peel and ginger until it has cooled down, then remove them and cut the peel into thin julienne strips.

Add the juice of the orange to the cooked syrup.

Cut the knobs of ginger into slices and sprinkle among the pineapple. Pour on the syrup, scatter the orange peel over the top and chill until needed.

MOLTEN CHOCOLATE MOULDS

Just before this book went to press, we were given the most delicious hot chocolate mini-mountains at a post confirmation lunch at Milton Abbey School in Dorset. Thanks to Fiona for the recipe. They are rich in chocolate (Fairtrade, of course) but very practical; you can make them up to the baking stage even a day or two in advance and they only take 10–12 minutes in a hot oven. Fiona used metal dariole moulds; I used china ramekins (¼ pint/150ml capacity) which work equally well, though may take a little longer in the oven. Easy to multiply for larger numbers.

For 8 ramekins

12oz/350g Fairtrade dark chocolate
  (70 per cent cocoa at least)
2oz/50g butter
6oz/150g caster sugar
4 large eggs, beaten with a pinch of salt
1 tsp vanilla essence
2oz/50g plain flour
8 ramekins
baking parchment

Preheat the oven to Gas 6/400F/200C.

Cut 8 discs of parchment to fit the bases of the ramekins. Butter the ramekins and press a disc into each.

Melt the chocolate in a bowl, either in the microwave or over a small pan of boiling water. Cool slightly.

Cream butter and sugar together and beat in the eggs and vanilla. Add the flour and make into a thick smooth batter with the cooled chocolate. Divide between the ramekins. At this stage you can keep them in the fridge until needed.

Fifteen minutes before you need them, place the ramekins on a baking tray and put into the hot oven for 10–12 minutes, until the tops are slightly cracked. Turn each out onto a warmed plate or bowl, remove the paper and serve with crème fraîche, thick yogurt or soured cream. There will be hot chocolate lava inside each mountain.

SEVILLE CHOCOLATE MOUSSE ☺

Seville oranges are one of the very few fruits still strictly seasonal and all the more appreciated for that. However, I usually freeze two or three oranges so that I can make this mousse at other seasons. Bitter orange and chocolate is a classic combination. Try serving the mousse from a large white bowl rather than individual ramekins.

For 10–12

12oz/350g Fairtrade dark chocolate
finely grated rind and juice of 2 Seville oranges
12 eggs, separated

Melt the chocolate, broken in pieces, in the microwave or in a bowl set over boiling water. Stir in the juice and rind of the oranges. Add the egg yolks, beaten, and stir all together. Remove from the heat. Whisk the egg whites with a pinch of salt till stiff and fold them carefully into the chocolate mixture with a metal spoon, making sure they are thoroughly incorporated without losing too much air.

Pour into the serving bowl and keep in a cool place till ready to serve. It improves with up to 48 hours' standing.

Summer

June, July, August

Summer and salads go together. Choose recipes which don't entail too much slaving over stoves, and take time out in the long light evenings to enjoy summer sounds and smells in gardens and parks. Enjoy summer fruits at their best: strawberries, raspberries and currants of all colours. Feed foreign friends on the best British produce and amaze and delight them.

Summer

Soups and Starters

Chillied Tomato Soup
Crème Vichyssoise – see page 58
Watercress Soup
Chicken Liver Parfait
Piedmont Roasted Peppers
Pea Puffs

Main Courses

Chicken and Melon Salad
Ham Baked with Apricots
Minty Lamb Stew
V Stuffed Peppers
V Gruyère Salad Roulade
V Layered Vegetable Terrine
How to Cook a Whole Salmon
Fish Goulash
Jamie's Tray-baked Salmon

Puddings

Gooseberry Fool
Yogurt and Cream Delight
Summer Fruits Wine Jelly
Lemon Flummery
Raspberry and Blackcurrant Chiffon Pie
Judy's Fruit Brûlée
Summer Fruit Meringue Roulade
Summer Pudding

Soups and Starters

CHILLIED TOMATO SOUP

Late one summer, when there was a glut of tomatoes, I planned to make a soup which could be had hot or cold, according to the weather. A creamy tomato soup. When the day came, the weather was fine but my soup tasted disappointingly insipid and even more so when cold. So at the last minute, in desperation, I added a good splash of chilli sauce and the effect on the cold creamy soup was unexpectedly good. Here is the simple recipe.

For 6–8

2lb/450g ripe tomatoes
3 medium onions, chopped
6oz/175g young carrots, chopped
3 pints/1.7 litres light stock, meat or vegetable
bouquet garni (bay leaf, thyme and parsley)
salt and pepper
a little sugar
½ pint/280ml single cream
½–1 dessertspoon chilli sauce

For 20

4lb/900g ripe tomatoes
6 medium onions, chopped
12oz/350g young carrots, chopped
5–6 pints/2.8–3.4 litres light stock, meat or vegetable
2 × bouquet garnis (bay leaf, thyme and parsley)
salt and pepper
a little sugar
1 pint/570ml single cream
1–2 dessertspoons chilli sauce

Simply put all the vegetables with the stock and the bouquet garni in a large saucepan, bring to the boil, cover and simmer till the vegetables are tender. Remove the bouquet, put the soup in the blender in batches and whiz until smooth, or put through a sieve. Taste and add seasoning accordingly. Stir in the cream and the chilli sauce and chill.

If you want to serve it hot, reheat after blending, stir in the cream and add rather less chilli.

Note: The advantage of sieving rather than whizzing is that you lose the tomato pips, which can taste bitter. But for large numbers, life may be too short.

WATERCRESS SOUP

We have been lucky to live in watercress-growing counties – Hampshire and Wiltshire – for over 25 years. It makes a lovely green soup, equally delicious hot or cold.

For 6–8	*For 20*
2 bunches watercress	4–5 bunches watercress
1 onion, chopped	2–3 onions, chopped
2oz/50g butter or margarine	4oz/110g butter or margarine
¾lb/350g potatoes, peeled and chopped	2lb/900g potatoes, peeled and chopped
1½ pints/900ml light stock or water	3 pints/1.7 litres light stock or water
¾ pint/450ml milk	3 pints/1.2 litres milk
salt and pepper	salt and pepper
¼ pint/150ml single cream	½ pint/300ml single cream
chopped chives (for cold soup)	chopped chives (for cold soup)

Wash the watercress and remove damaged leaves. Chop leaves and stalks together. Sweat the onion in the melted butter for a few minutes, add the watercress and cook gently together for 5 minutes more. Then add the chopped potatoes and the stock or water and cook until tender. Liquidise (or sieve) the soup, return to the pan and stir in the milk, bringing it all to the boil. Taste and add salt and pepper if necessary and stir in the cream before serving.

To serve cold, cool the soup before adding the cream, chill and stir in the cream with some chopped chives before serving.

CHICKEN LIVER PARFAIT

! 2–3 hours' soaking needed

This wonderfully rich pâté is unexpectedly economical because chicken livers are so absurdly cheap. (Unfortunately it doesn't seem possible to buy free-range livers: I wonder what happens to them?) It stretches a long way; serve with Melba toast as a special starter.

Another Sainsbury recipe from Josceline Dimbleby (*Festive Food and Party Pieces*, 1982).

For 6–8	*For 20*
8oz/225g chicken livers	1lb/450g chicken livers
milk to cover	milk to cover
6oz/175g unsalted butter	12oz/350g unsalted butter
1 Tbsp dry sherry	2 Tbsp dry sherry
5fl oz/150ml double cream	10fl oz/300ml double cream
a good pinch of caster sugar	2 pinches of caster sugar
salt and black pepper	salt and black pepper
lettuce leaves, thin slices of lemon, sprigs of parsley to garnish	lettuce leaves, thin slices of lemon, sprigs of parsley to garnish

Put the chicken livers in a bowl and cover with milk. Leave them in the fridge to soak for 2–3 hours, then drain.

Melt the butter in a saucepan, add the drained livers, season with salt and pepper and cook gently, stirring them over and over in the open pan for about 10 minutes. Leave until completely cold, then pulverise in a blender or food processor until smooth. Gradually blend in the sherry, then scrape it all out into a bowl.

Whisk the cream until thick but not stiff. Stir it thoroughly into the liver purée with a wooden spoon. Add the sugar, and season to taste with salt and pepper. Spoon into a 1 pint/600ml round or oval dish and smooth the top. Refrigerate.

When ready to serve, dip the dish in very hot water and turn out onto a serving plate. Smooth it all over with the flat blade of a knife. Garnish with sprigs of parsley and surround with lettuce leaves and thin slices of lemon. Serve with Melba toast or thin toast.

Note: This keeps well, so you can make it 2–3 days ahead, unmoulding it on the day.

PIEDMONT ROASTED PEPPERS

This recipe, discovered first by Elizabeth David and used by many chefs over the years, is described by Delia Smith in her *Summer Collection* (BBC Books 1993). It makes a wonderful starter to a summer or autumn feast. Remember that if you make 3 times the basic recipe, it will take you 3 times as long, so allow plenty of time. Try to choose large, plump peppers, so that a half will make a good starter.

For 6–8

4 large, plump peppers (red, yellow or orange – not green)
4 medium tomatoes
8 tinned anchovy fillets, drained
2 fat cloves garlic, peeled
8 dessertspoons best olive oil
freshly milled black pepper
some fresh basil leaves to serve

Preheat the oven to Gas 4/350F/180C.

Cut the peppers in half lengthwise, keeping a half stalk on each half. Remove the seeds. Lay the pepper halves in a shallow, oiled roasting tray.

Put the tomatoes in a bowl and cover with boiling water. Take a fork and spear each in turn, slipping the skins off. Cut them in quarters lengthways and put 2 quarters in each pepper half.

Now snip the anchovy fillets over the tomatoes in each half. Slice the garlic thinly and divide among the tomatoes and the anchovies.

Spoon 1 dessertspoon of olive oil into each pepper, season with black pepper (no salt because of the anchovies) and put the tray on a high shelf in the oven for 50–60 minutes.

Transfer to a serving dish with all the juices poured over and garnish with some basil leaves.

Serve warm or cool with lots of crusty bread.

PEA PUFFS

Another brilliant recipe from Josceline Dimbleby (*Salads for all Seasons*, Sainsbury 1981) which makes a very good starter for a special summer party. Not to be eaten in the hand, unless you make miniature ones. They look impressive and taste wonderful but are not difficult to make.

You do need a strong arm for the puffs, and a liquidiser for the filling.

For 6–8 (makes about 20)

5oz/150g plain flour
1 tsp salt
½ tsp cayenne pepper
½ pint/280ml water
4oz/110g butter
3 large eggs
4oz/110g Gruyère cheese, grated

For the filling

1lb/450g frozen peas
a large handful of fresh mint leaves
4 Tbsp single cream
½–1 whole nutmeg, grated
salt and black pepper
6–8fl oz/175–225ml good quality mayonnaise

For 20 (makes about 60)

15oz/450g plain flour
3 tsp salt
1½ tsp cayenne pepper
1½ pints/850ml water
12oz/350g butter
9 large eggs
12oz/350g Gruyère cheese, grated

For the filling

3lb/1.35kg frozen peas
3 large handfuls of fresh mint leaves
12 Tbsp single cream
1½ whole nutmegs, grated
salt and black pepper
1 pint/570ml good quality mayonnaise

To make the puffs, sift the flour, salt and cayenne pepper into a bowl. Bring the water and butter to the boil in a large heavy saucepan, stirring until the butter melts. When it boils, tip in all the flour at once and beat with a wooden spoon until smooth (still over the heat). Continue beating vigorously until the mixture leaves the side of the pan.

Remove from the heat and beat in the eggs, one at a time, beating thoroughly between each. Continue until the mixture is smooth and glossy. Beat in all but 1oz/25g of the cheese (3oz/80g for the larger quantity).

Preheat the oven to Gas 7/425F/220C. Grease a large baking tray and spoon on dessertspoons of the mixture, a little apart. Sprinkle the rest of the cheese over the top of the puffs. Bake in the centre of the oven for 25–30 minutes until well risen and golden. Remove carefully and cool on a rack.

Meanwhile, to make the filling, cook the frozen peas, drain and rinse with cold water. Put them in the liquidiser with the mint leaves and cream. Whiz to a thick mush – not completely smooth. Season generously with the nutmeg, salt and pepper, tasting as you go. Transfer to a bowl and mix in the mayonnaise.

When the puffs are cold, slit them open horizontally, leaving one side attached as a hinge, and spoon the pea mayonnaise into them.

Serve on individual plates or on a large dish, decorated with lettuce leaves.

Note: If you've not made profiteroles before, do have a go – it is much easier than you think and needs strength of arm rather than lightness of touch.

Main Courses

CHICKEN AND MELON SALAD

☺ (if chicken is already cooked)

When I asked my fellow bishops' wives for recipes suitable for this book, Judith Nicholls sent this one from Sheffield. It is, as she says, quick and easy, very popular and has a delightfully refreshing taste.

For 6–8	*For 20*
1 cooked free-range chicken, cut into bite-size pieces (see note)	2 cooked free-range chicken, cut into bite-size pieces (see note)
1 large honeydew melon, cut in pieces	2 large honeydew melons, cut in pieces
½ pint/280ml low fat mayonnaise	1 pint/570ml low fat mayonnaise
½ pint/280ml organic yogurt	1 pint/570ml organic yogurt
6–8 Tbsp mango chutney	12 Tbsp mango chutney
1 large red pepper, cut in strips	2 large red peppers, cut in strips

Mix the chicken and melon together in a serving dish. Mix together the mayonnaise, yogurt and chutney in a bowl, spoon it over the chicken and melon and mix all well together. Decorate with strips of red pepper. Serve with salads and crusty bread.

Note: If you are cooking the chicken yourself, you can either roast it or boil it. If you roast it, keep the frizzly skin on when you cut it up – it will add to the flavour. If you boil it, the skin will be less attractive and should be discarded. But the stock will be well worth keeping for soups and sauces. You can, of course, buy ready-roasted chicken to save time but they are not usually free-range.

HAM BAKED WITH APRICOTS

! if you soak your ham – see recipe

I always used to boil large pieces of ham in lots of water with onion, carrot and bay leaf and then skin and glaze them with mustard and sugar in a hot oven for 20–30 minutes. This method is fine and gives you gallons of ham stock but there is another, easier method which you might like to try.

Most gammon these days does not strictly need soaking but for this method of cooking it is worth soaking it for a few hours, or bringing it to the boil and then draining off the water and throwing it away. This is because you are not going to use any water, and the apricots will pick up the salt which the ham exudes as it cooks.

For 25–30

12–14lb/5.4–6.3kg boned, rolled ham
1lb Fairtrade dried apricots
6 bay leaves
½ pint/300ml cider or white wine
French mustard
brown sugar

For the sauce
½ pint/300ml cider or wine
2 tsp cornflour
water

Preheat the oven to Gas 3/325F/170C.

Lay a double layer of foil in a large roasting tin, leaving enough foil over to enclose the whole ham.

Put the apricots all over the bottom of the foil, lay the ham on top, tuck the bay leaves around, pour in the cider or wine and close up the foil, leaving room for steam inside.

Bake in the middle of the oven for about 5 hours, testing by opening the foil and piercing the ham with a skewer right to the middle – if there is little or no resistance, it is done.

Unwrap the ham while it is hot, skin, and score the fat in a criss-cross pattern. Spread a paste of mustard and brown sugar over it and brown in a hotter oven – Gas 6/400F/200C – for 20 minutes.

Purée the apricots with some of the cooking liquid, then taste the result for saltiness. Heat the cider or wine in a small pan, slake the cornflour in a little water and add that to the pan, stir and let it thicken slightly. Then add the salty apricot purée gradually, stopping when the flavour is right for you.

Serve the ham hot, a little sauce on each helping, with new potatoes and broad beans and parsley.

Or let the joint cool, carve when cold and use the apricot purée as a salty relish.

MINTY LAMB STEW ☺

This lamb stew is fresh-tasting, very simple to make and always popular. I used to make it with scrag end and other cheap bony pieces of lamb but for larger numbers it is better to buy meat off the bone; get your butcher to cut you up some pieces of shoulder.

It comes from Josceline Dimbleby's *Family Meat and Fish Cookery* (Sainsbury 1979).

For 6–8	*For 20*
2–2½lb/800g–1.15kg stewing lamb	5–6lb/2.25–2.7kg stewing lamb
3 large onions, sliced in rings	9 large onions, sliced in rings
3 large ripe tomatoes, skinned and chopped *or* 1 × 14oz/400g tin tomatoes, chopped	9 large ripe tomatoes, skinned and chopped *or* 3 × 14oz/400g tins tomatoes, chopped
large handful of fresh mint, chopped	plenty of fresh mint, chopped
juice of 1½ lemons	juice of 3 lemons
1 pint/600ml good stock	3 pints/1.7 litres good stock
salt and black pepper	salt and black pepper

Preheat the oven to Gas 3/325F/170C.

Put all the ingredients into a large ovenproof casserole. Cover, bring to the boil on top of the stove and simmer in the oven for 1½–2 hours, till the meat is tender.

Serve with rice or boiled potatoes and carrots or a green vegetable.

STUFFED PEPPERS

Choose the brightest coloured peppers for this recipe – red, yellow and orange – which are sweeter than the green, and try to find ones that will stand upright in the baking dish. These peppers make an excellent vegetarian alternative at a party; you should be able to fit 6–8 large peppers in a large roasting pan. They are also good-tempered and will keep warm for hours in the lowest oven, or reheat if you make them in advance. Bulghur is easier than rice as it just needs soaking but it does need vigorous seasoning.

For 6–8

10oz/275g bulghur wheat
6–8 large sweet peppers
2 Tbsp olive oil
1 large onion, chopped finely
1–2 cloves garlic, chopped finely
2–3 firm mushrooms, chopped
a large handful of parsley, chopped
1 Tbsp pine nuts
2 Tbsp Fairtrade raisins
2 ripe tomatoes, chopped
salt, pepper and cayenne pepper

First, put the bulghur wheat in a large bowl and soak it plenty of cold water for 30 minutes. Meanwhile, bring a large pan of salted water to the boil. Cut the top from each pepper and scoop out the seeds and the pith from inside. Plunge the peppers, and their lids, into boiling water and parboil them for 5 minutes, just to soften them a little. Drain well and set them side by side in a well-oiled ovenproof dish or roasting pan.

Preheat the oven to Gas 4/350F/180C. Heat the oil in a large frying pan and soften the onion over a medium heat with the garlic. Add the chopped mushroom, parsley, pine nuts and raisins and fry them all together. Turn the heat down and stir in the drained bulghur and the chopped tomatoes, mixing it all well. Remove from the heat and season well with salt, ground black pepper and a pinch or two of cayenne.

Fill the peppers with the mixture and put the lids back on, drizzle with a little more oil and bake in the oven for 30–40 minutes, till the peppers are tender and the tops blackened.

Serve warm or cold.

GRUYÈRE SALAD ROULADE

This is a party dish aimed at vegetarians but enjoyed by everybody. It is another of Josceline Dimbleby's wonderful inventions (from *Salads for all Seasons*, Sainsbury 1981). The lettuce, tomato and mushroom filling can be varied if other vegetables are in season. It is worth buying real Gruyère for this recipe – the other ingredients are not extravagant. To feed more than 6–8 people you will need to duplicate the whole recipe.

For 6–8

a little grated Parmesan
2oz/50g fresh white breadcrumbs
6oz/175g Gruyère cheese, finely grated
4 eggs, separated
¼ pint/150ml single cream
2 Tbsp warm water
4–5 Tbsp mayonnaise
¼–½ a crisp lettuce, shredded
2–3 tomatoes, finely sliced
1oz/25g mushrooms, finely sliced
1 Tbsp fresh chives or mint, chopped
salt, pepper and cayenne

Preheat the oven to Gas 6/400F/200C. Line a shallow baking tray (13 × 9in/33 × 23cm) with baking parchment and sprinkle with a little grated Parmesan. Mix breadcrumbs and Gruyère together in a bowl, add the egg yolks and cream and season with salt and 2–3 pinches of cayenne. Stir in the warm water to slacken the mixture.

Whisk the egg whites with a pinch of salt until they stand in soft peaks, then fold them gently into the cream mixture with a metal spoon. Pour into the baking tray.

Bake in the centre of the oven for 10–15 minutes, till risen and firm to the touch. Remove and cool slightly – it will shrink a bit but don't worry. Wring out a clean tea cloth in cold water and lay it on top of the roulade. Leave to cool completely, then loosen the edges with a knife.

Sprinkle another sheet of parchment with grated Parmesan and turn the roulade out onto the paper. Spread generously with mayonnaise, then spread out the shredded lettuce, sliced tomatoes and mushrooms and herbs on top, as evenly as possible. Season with a little salt and plenty of ground black pepper.

Now roll up, fairly loosely, with the help of the paper. Transfer carefully to a serving dish. To serve, cut in slices like a Swiss roll.

Note: If you vary the filling, remember to include something crunchy and something juicy. It is one of the few recipes where I think iceberg lettuce comes into its own.

LAYERED VEGETABLE TERRINE

Summer brings sunshine, with luck, and buffet parties to tempt and delight the palate. This vegetable terrine is easy to make and you can vary the vegetables so long as the colours are contrasting.

The basic recipe feeds 6–8; for larger numbers you can simply line up 1 or 2 more loaf tins and make 2 or 3 times the basic recipe.

For 6–8

1lb/450g carrots, chopped
6 large free-range eggs
1lb/450g cauliflower florets
2 Tbsp fresh coriander, chopped
1lb/450g spinach
nutmeg to grate
3 Tbsp single cream
salt and pepper

Lightly oil a 2lb/1kg loaf tin. Preheat the oven to Gas 6/400F/200C. Put the carrots and cauliflower into separate pans with boiling salted water and cook until just tender. Drain and purée them separately, add 2 beaten eggs to each and stir half the cream into the carrot purée and all the coriander into the cauliflower. Season both to taste.

Now cook the spinach in a little salted water, drain well, beat in the remaining 2 eggs and the rest of the cream and season with nutmeg. Taste and add more salt and pepper if need be.

Spread the carrot purée over the base of the tin, then the cauliflower layer and finally the spinach. Stand the tin in a roasting pan half full of hot water and bake in the oven for 1½ hours. Allow to cool before turning out and serve warm or cold.

Note: For winter variations you could use broccoli instead of spinach and Jerusalem artichokes instead of cauliflower.

HOW TO COOK A WHOLE SALMON

Few of us can find or afford wild salmon but good fresh farmed salmon is well worth buying for a large summer party. By June or July the supply is usually good and they are often sold at half price. Salmon is very filling – a 5lb/2.3kg fish will feed at least 12 people; allow a 10lb/4.5kg fish for 20–25 guests, maybe 30 if it is part of a mixed buffet. It may be easier to cook two 5lb fish rather than one larger one.

For eating cold, you can either poach or bake your salmon. In either case, begin by tearing off a piece of strong foil large enough to enclose the whole fish. Lay it flat and oil it all over. Lay the fish on it and season well with salt and pepper. Now bring the foil up around the fish, not too tight so that there is room for steam inside, and fold the edges of the foil together to make an airtight seal.

To poach

If you have (or can borrow) a fish kettle long enough for your salmon, then place your baggy parcel of fish in the kettle, add cold water to within 1in/2.5cm of the top and bring it to the boil. Count slowly to five, remove the kettle from the heat and let the fish cool in its wrappings in the water. Whatever the size of the salmon, it will be perfectly cooked, nice and moist. (It makes sense – the larger the fish, the longer it takes to heat up and cool down, so the longer the cooking it gets.)

Note: You can achieve a delightfully curved salmon by poaching the parcel in a large round casserole, bending it to fit the pan.

To bake

Preheat the oven to Gas 1/275F/140C or use the lowest Aga oven. Bake the parcel on a baking tray allowing 1 hour for a fish up to 5lb/2.3kg and 12 minutes per pound/450g for anything over that.

To test whether the fish is cooked, undo the foil enough to try lifting a piece of skin with the blade of a small knife. If it comes away easily, the salmon is cooked.

For hot salmon, use the baking method, let it stand for 10 minutes after you've removed it from the oven, skin and serve with hollandaise sauce or a **simple cream sauce with herbs**: melt 8oz/225g unsalted butter gently in a frying pan, add 10fl oz/280ml double cream, turn up the heat and bubble till it thickens – 2 or 3 minutes. Season with salt, pepper and lemon juice and stir in 3 Tbsp chopped fresh herbs – tarragon, chives, parsley or whatever. This quantity will serve 10–12 portions.

Serve cold salmon, skinned and decorated with slices of cucumber, lemon and some prawns if possible, with plenty of good mayonnaise or a **cold herby cream sauce**: mix 4 Tbsp chopped dill and 4 Tbsp chopped parsley into 5fl oz/150ml crème fraîche and 10fl oz/280ml good mayonnaise. Add 2 Tbsp lemon juice, season with salt and pepper and mix all well together. This can be made 2–3 days in advance and refrigerated. Enough for 10–12 portions.

Suitable salads to accompany the salmon would be the spicy Green Pea Salad (see page 198), Tomato Salad and Green Salad (see page 193). Hot new potatoes rolled in butter and parsley go well.

FISH GOULASH

This goulash – so called because of the peppers, the paprika and the final addition of yogurt – is a very useful dish because you can make the vegetable base a day or two before and add the fish only 20 minutes before serving. From *Delicious Fish* by Claire Macdonald (Grafton 1999).

For 6–8	*For 20*
3 Tbsp olive oil	5 Tbsp olive oil
2 medium onions, sliced	6 medium onions, sliced
3 red and 2 green peppers, seeded and chopped	12–15 mixed peppers, seeded and chopped
6 ripe tomatoes, skinned, seeded and chopped	12 ripe tomatoes, skinned, seeded and chopped
1 Tbsp tomato purée	2 Tbsp tomato purée
2 tsp paprika	4 tsp paprika
½ tsp sugar	1 tsp sugar
salt and pepper	salt and pepper
2lb/900g firm white fish, filleted	5–6lb/2.3–2.7kg firm white fish, filleted
¼ pint/150ml plain yogurt	½ pint/300ml plain yogurt

Heat the oil in a large casserole, add the onions and soften over gentle heat for 5 minutes or so, stirring. Add the peppers and cook for another 5 minutes, stirring from time to time. Add the tomatoes, purée, paprika, sugar and seasoning (plenty of pepper) and cook, uncovered, for 30 minutes. Stir to stop it burning; the stew should thicken nicely. All this can be done in advance.

Half an hour before the meal, reheat the stew over a moderate heat, stirring to prevent sticking. Cut the fish into 1in/2.5cm pieces. Add the fish to the casserole, cover and simmer for 15–20 minutes. Check that the fish is cooked through. Pour the yogurt over just before serving.

Rice or boiled potatoes go well with this, and a green salad.

JAMIE'S TRAY-BAKED SALMON

This dish comes from one of Jamie Oliver's early books and is a really good way of serving salmon steaks to lots of people.

For 6–8	*For 20*
12oz/350g green beans	2lb/1kg green beans
1lb/450g (30) cherry tomatoes	2½lb/1.2kg cherry tomatoes
2 good handfuls of black olives, stoned	4 good handfuls of black olives, stoned
3 Tbsp olive oil	6 Tbsp olive oil
salt and black pepper	salt and black pepper
1 small lemon, halved	3 small lemons, halved
a handful of basil leaves	a handful of basil leaves
2 tins of anchovy fillets	4 tins of anchovy fillets
6–8 × 6–8oz/175–225g salmon steaks, boned and skinned	20 × 6oz/175g salmon steaks, boned and skinned
lemon quarters to serve	lemon quarters to serve

Tail the beans, blanch them until tender in salted boiling water and drain. Put them in a bowl with the tomatoes and the stoned olives. Toss in the olive oil and season with a little salt and grind of black pepper.

Preheat the oven to very high – Gas 9/475F/240C – and heat a roasting tray (2 large ones for the larger quantity) in it. Add the basil, torn in pieces, to the beans and tomatoes and spread them over the bottom of the roasting tray. Lay the anchovy fillets over the top.

Now wipe the salmon fillets with a clean damp cloth, squeeze a little lemon juice over each side, season with salt and pepper on both sides, lay them on top of the bean mixture and drizzle olive oil over the top.

Roast in the hot oven for 10 minutes, until the fish is just cooked through.

Serve with crusty bread or new potatoes and perhaps some homemade mayonnaise (see page 222).

Note: If cherry tomatoes are not to hand, use the best flavoured larger tomatoes you can find and cut them into pieces.

Puddings

GOOSEBERRY FOOL

If you grow gooseberries, this will be one of your mainstay summer party puddings. When our son wanted it for a late June wedding feast, I made pints of mashed fruit and froze it till the wedding eve, so that all I had to do was whip the cream and fold it in. We like the gooseberries mashed rather than finely puréed – you can choose.

For 10–12

2lb/900g gooseberries, topped and tailed
2 Tbsp water
6–8oz/160–225g Fairtrade caster sugar
1 Tbsp elderflower cordial (see recipe, page 219)
1 pint/600ml double or whipping cream or a mixture

Cook the gooseberries with the water in a covered pan over a gentle heat until the fruit breaks or is tender. Take off the heat, crush the fruit with a potato masher (or purée in a blender or sieve it if you prefer, but the flavour will not be so good) and stir in the sugar to taste and the tablespoon of elderflower cordial.

When it is cool, whip the cream (or creams) until thick but not stiff and fold into the gooseberry mush. Serve from a pretty bowl – pink if possible.

Note: Elderflower goes well with gooseberry; if you can find them, put a couple of heads of elderflower (insects shaken out) to cook with the fruit and omit the cordial. Extract the flowers before you mash.

YOGURT AND CREAM DELIGHT ☺

! needs to stand for several hours

Many party puddings need time and care to make; this one takes only a few minutes to assemble but stands very well as a complement to fruit salads and chocolate tarts alike, so it is a real delight. Thanks again to Louise.

For 10–12

1 pint/570ml whipping or double cream or a mixture
1 pint/570ml Greek-style yogurt
8oz/225g Fairtrade dark muscovado sugar

Whip the cream until it is the same consistency as the yogurt. Fold the cream into the yogurt in a large mixing bowl.

Take a serving bowl, glass if possible, and put half the cream mixture in the bottom. Sprinkle half the sugar over it, then spoon the rest of the cream over the sugar. Use the remaining sugar to cover the top of the cream and leave in a cool place to stand for several hours, to allow the sugar to begin to dissolve into the cream.

You can easily vary the amount of this pudding as long as the proportions of yogurt to sugar remain the same. The number of mouths it will feed will depend on how many other puddings are offered alongside.

SUMMER FRUITS WINE JELLY

This recipe came to me from a catering friend but I think has Delia origins: it is a brilliant way to serve fresh summer fruit by setting them in a sharp tasting jelly. This means you can make it several days before the party and keep it in the fridge. Although sparkling wine is specified (and it keeps its sparkle in the jelly), any cheap rosé or light red wine will do the job.

Note: You need a 2lb/900g loaf tin, and ideally a second one to fit inside to weigh down the jelly. Because the quantities given fit nicely into the tin, it is not a recipe to augment for larger numbers – unless you decide to make a second jelly (and so need 4 tins). But it is a very good pudding to serve alongside others. See afterthought, below.

For 8

1½lb/700g fresh fruit: strawberries, raspberries, black and redcurrants, blueberries, in whatever proportion you like – bear in mind that blackcurrants can easily predominate
15fl oz/425ml rosé or red wine, still or sparkling
2 × 0.4oz/10g sachets or 2 level Tbsp gelatine
2oz/50g caster sugar
juice of 1 small lime

Pick over and clean the fruit but don't get it wet. Heat half the wine in a small pan and, *keeping it below boiling point*, whisk in the sugar and gelatine. Go on whisking until the gelatine dissolves, then take off the heat and add the rest of the wine and 1 tablespoon of lime juice and leave to cool. Taste and add more lime juice if need be.

Take a 2lb/900g loaf tin, preferably non-stick, and lay the fruit in the tin, remembering that the fruit you place on the bottom will eventually turn out as the top layer, so choose the best fruit first.

Pour the cooled gelatine mixture over the fruit – it should come nearly to the top of the tin. Leave in a cool place to set.

When it is set, cover the surface with clingfilm and set the second tin on top and just inside, weighing it down with a couple of tins of beans or suchlike. The point of weighing it down is to make the jelly as firm as possible for cutting. (I didn't have a second tin of the right shape so improvised with two fruit punnets, putting a weight in each; this meant a ridge appeared between them, but when I turned it out the ridge was invisible underneath.) Refrigerate until needed.

Loosen the edge of the jelly with a knife, run the hot tap quickly over the bottom of the tin and turn the jelly out onto a serving dish.

Serve in slices with or without cream.

Afterthought: For larger numbers, you could forgo loaf tins altogether and simply make the augmented jelly in a large white bowl and spoon it out instead of cutting slices. Much less trouble and should still taste good.

LEMON FLUMMERY

This is the first cold pudding I learned to make – it is economical and easy, though you need a little patience to let the mixture thicken properly as you stir. The finished effort is like a moist lemon soufflé; most people guess there is cream in it but in fact the ingredients are everyday ones. If you use margarine instead of butter, it could be dairy-free.

For 8–10

2oz/50g plain flour
8oz/225g Fairtrade granulated sugar
1 pint/570ml water
2oz/50g butter or margarine
grated rind and juice of 2 large or 4 small lemons
4 free-range eggs, separated, yolks beaten

Mix the flour and sugar in a large bowl. Bring to the boil water, butter, lemon rind and juice in a large saucepan, removing it from the heat once the butter has melted.

Add the liquid gradually to the dry mixture in the bowl, stirring all the time. Add the beaten egg yolks and mix thoroughly. Return it all to the saucepan and cook over low heat to thicken for about 15 minutes, stirring all the time. (A high kitchen stool can help the aching legs.)

Remove from the heat and cool for half an hour or so. Whisk the egg-whites until stiff and then fold gently but thoroughly into the lemon mixture.

Pour into a pretty serving bowl and store in the fridge until needed.

RASPBERRY AND BLACKCURRANT CHIFFON PIE

This recipe, for a light and tangy but creamy summer pie, comes from Christine who commissioned this book. She says you can use half and half raspberries and blackcurrants but we both think it's best in a 3:1 ratio because blackcurrants have such a strong flavour and the raspberries need to shine.

For 10

For the biscuit base

6oz/150g digestive biscuits
3oz/75g butter
1½ Tbsp Fairtrade demerara sugar

For the filling

juice of ½ lemon, made up to 3 Tbsp with water
1 sachet (0.4oz/10g) or 4 leaves gelatine
8oz/225g fruit (6oz/150g raspberries and
  2oz/50g blackcurrants)
4oz/100g Fairtrade caster sugar
1 free-range egg white
½ pint/300ml double cream

To decorate

a few raspberries and mint leaves

Lightly oil a 9in/23cm spring-form or loose-bottomed flan tin. Put the biscuits in a polythene bag and crush with a rolling pin.

Melt the butter in a pan and stir in the biscuit crumbs and sugar. Press into the base of the tin and refrigerate.

Put the lemon juice and water into a small bowl and sprinkle over the gelatine (or immerse the leaves). Leave to go spongy. Put the fruit and half the caster sugar in a pan and heat gently until the sugar dissolves. Add the gelatine mixture and stir until dissolved. Remove from heat and leave to cool.

Whisk the egg white till stiff, add the rest of the sugar gradually, beating as you go, until smooth and shiny. In another bowl lightly whip up the cream.

When the fruit mixture is on the point of setting, stir in the cream and fold in the whipped egg white. Pour into the flan tin and return to the fridge to set for 2–3 hours.

To serve, remove from the tin and decorate with raspberries and mint leaves.

JUDY'S FRUIT BRÛLÉE

! You need a flame gun, borrowed if necessary, for this recipe. Allow 12 hours for chilling.

This wonderful pudding can be done for 2 or 20; the size of your gratin dish will determine the number. Judy, who makes this superbly, has an oval dish of 6½ pints/4 litres capacity, which feeds about 15. My own largest dish takes 5 pints/3 litres and will feed 10–12. It is a very popular party choice, so you may need to make two.

For 10–12

soft fruit, enough to fill two-thirds of the chosen dish – 2–3lb/1–1½ kg for a 5 pint/3 litre dish – raspberries, strawberries, loganberries, blackberries, redcurrants, blackcurrants (not too many), kiwi, mangoes, nectarines, plums, bananas, pears, grapes, blueberries (choose a variety of colours and flavours)
1 pint/600ml double cream
1 pint/600ml Greek-style yogurt
6–8oz/150–225g Fairtrade granulated sugar (*not* caster)

Put the fruit in the gratin dish to come two-thirds of the way up. Whip the cream and yogurt together until thick and doubled in volume. Spread over the fruit and chill in the fridge for 12 hours or so.

Sprinkle thickly with the granulated sugar and use a flame gun to burn the sugar until liquid and bubbling brown. Return immediately to the fridge for a couple of hours until ready to serve.

Note: You can use a very hot grill to caramelise the sugar but the result will be patchy and the grill very sticky.

SUMMER FRUIT MERINGUE ROULADE

There are endless variations on the roulade theme; this is a simple summer version. Once you have grasped the basic recipe, you can invent your own.

For 10–12

5 large free-range eggs, separated
8oz/225g Fairtrade caster sugar
1 tsp cornflour
¾ pint/450ml double cream
1lb/450g raspberries, strawberries, blueberries or a mixture

Preheat the oven to Gas 5/375F/190C and cover your baking tray with parchment paper and sprinkle with icing sugar.

Whisk the egg yolks and sugar together to the 'ribbon' stage (see page 42). Whisk the whites separately with the cornflour and fold into the yolk mixture. Spread onto the parchment and bake in the centre of the oven for about 20 minutes till firm. Remove and cover with a clean cloth till cool.

Whip the cream, spread it over the roulade, cover with the fruits and roll up from a short end. Serve from a large oval platter.

Note: Lemon curd makes a good alternative to cream, with or without fruit. You could use light brown sugar for the roulade and fill it with pineapple and chopped ginger.

SUMMER PUDDING

! best chilled overnight

This is such a simple idea – bread and soft fruits – but so delicious and always a hit, especially with foreign guests who have never met it before. It freezes very well, so you could make several small ones and have unexpected treats in the winter months.

Plastic bowls with lids are ideal and usually have their capacity marked on the bottom. You will need a 2–2½ pint/1–1.5 litre bowl for these quantities. Use good-quality white bread at least a day old. Loganberries and mulberries are unusual but very good in summer puddings if you can get them.

For 6–8

2–2½lb/900g–1.5kg soft fruit, e.g. raspberries, redcurrants, blackcurrants, loganberries, mulberries, blueberries
7oz/190g Fairtrade granulated sugar
9–10 slices white bread from a large loaf, crusts removed

Put the fruit and sugar into a saucepan, cover and heat gently, shaking the pan so nothing sticks. Cook for a few minutes only, just until the fruit lets out its juice and the sugar melts. Cover the base and sides of the bowl with bread, cutting the bread to measure so there are no gaps.

Now spoon all the fruit into the bowl, reserving just a small cup of the juice. Cover completely with more bread, find a small plate or saucer to fit exactly inside the rim of the bowl, weigh it down with a couple of heavy tins or a 2–3lb/900g–1.3kg weight and leave overnight in the fridge.

To serve, run a knife around the top edge of the pudding, put a deepish serving plate on top, upend it and shake briskly to turn it out. Use the reserved cup of juice to pour all over it (there are often small patches of white left) and serve in slices with thick cream beside.

Note: A very large pudding (4–5 pints/2.3–2.8 litres) might collapse, so it would be better to make 2 smaller ones.

Seasonal Vegetables and Salads

Selecting your Fillers and Vegetables

Autumn into Winter – Hot Vegetables

Ragoût of Peppers and Onions
Runner Beans
Carrot and Swede Mash
Potato and Celeriac Mash
Braised Red Cabbage
Gratin Dauphinois
Braised Vegetables
Potatoes à la Boulangère
Ratatouille

Autumn into Winter – Salads

Mixed Bean Salad
Waldorf Salad
Aubergines in Yogurt
Carrot Salad
Chicory, Orange and Fennel Salad
Coleslaw

Spring into Summer – Hot Vegetables

Young Turnips
Broad Beans
New Potatoes
Leeks in a Sauce
Green Flageolet Beans with Cream
White Cabbage with Cumin

Spring into Summer – Salads

Potato Salad
Rice Salad
Pasta Salad
Tomato Salad
Green Salad
Marinated Minty Mushrooms
Tsatsiki
Bulghur Wheat Salad
Green Pea Salad with Ginger and Olives

Selecting your Fillers and Vegetables

Vegetables served alongside the main course at any party need careful thought; can they be prepared in advance without spoiling, will they complement the main dish in colour and taste and how much of each will be needed?

First the fillers: pasta, rice and potatoes.

Choose which is most suitable for your main course (a curry will need rice, a stew mashed potato perhaps) but do not serve a choice because you will have to cook much more of each than is needed. Pasta is the most tricky because it doesn't sit about happily and is best used for salads at cold buffets (see page 193) or in lasagnes.

Rice – Choose a good long grain rice such as Fairtrade basmati. Allow 2oz/50g per head – don't be tempted to cook more even though it doesn't look much – this will be enough! Boil in a copious saucepan – for 20 people you need 2½lb/1.15kg rice and about 16 pints/9 litres salted water. Use two pans if need be.

Boil fast for 10–12 minutes, till it is cooked but not mushy. Drain in a large colander, rinse through with very hot water, shake out the surplus and turn into a large serving dish. Fork it up and pop it into a low oven for a few minutes to dry. We often stir a knob or two of butter through it. Cover with a clean tea cloth and keep warm until needed. Reheating rice is not a brilliant idea for large numbers – there is a toxin called *bacillus cereus* which can cause illness if the reheating is not thorough.

Potatoes – Depending on the season, buy new or old. New can be steamed in their skins and rolled in butter, old can be mashed or baked (not too large), or cooked à la boulangère (see page 180) or in a Gratin Dauphinois (see page 178); keep roast potatoes for family or dinner parties.

Allow 6–8oz/160–225g per person, using the lower guide for large numbers. So for 20, cook 8lb/3.6kg potatoes. For mashing, allow slightly more because you lose some weight in the peeling and also people seem to eat more of it. Mashed potato needs a good lump of butter and a grind of black pepper and I prefer to beat in some of its cooking water rather than milk or cream, for a smooth but light texture.

Mashed potato can be kept warm in a very low oven, covered with foil or else uncovered to crisp slightly on top (see pages 177–8 for Potato and Celeriac Mash).

Now what to choose beside the filler? My advice is to keep delicate greens, such as purple sprouting broccoli, for dinner parties and family meals. For larger buffet meals and parties, choose among the more robust vegetables which will wait happily for when they are needed.

Among these are:

Red and white cabbage	Ideal for large numbers and will reheat and freeze (see pages 178 and 191).
Root vegetables	Carrots, swede, parsnips, Jerusalem artichokes either on their own or in ragoûts, or in purées (see Carrot and Swede Mash page 177). Among these, carrots win most often because of their colour and flavour. Dress boiled carrots with a lump of butter and a squeeze of lemon.
Green beans	French and runner beans – a useful green element. Do not overcook. Turn in butter with chopped parsley.

Mediterranean vegetables	Peppers, aubergines, courgettes. All of them good for parties, though courgettes tricky on their own as they can easily overcook (see Ratatouille, pages 181–2, and Ragoût of Peppers and Onions, page 177).
Tomatoes	Delicious halved and baked with garlic and parsley and breadcrumbs – not for huge numbers, though. More useful in salads (see Tomato Salad, page 193).
Spinach	Lovely stuff, but you need so much weight per person – about 12oz/350g – that it is not really practicable for large parties. But if you do have a glut, it is well worth cooking it, draining well, seasoning with salt and nutmeg and plenty of butter. It reheats beautifully, so you can prepare it even a day ahead.
Broad beans	Delicious fresh but also very good frozen and we use them often. A 2lb/900g bag of beans will feed 8–10 people, more if other vegetables are served. They combine well with carrots (mixed in after cooking); dress with butter and chopped parsley.
Calabrese	More practicable than purple sprouting for large numbers but needs cheering up. Cook till just tender in forkable pieces, then dress with breadcrumbs and garlic fried in olive oil and scattered over just before serving. Allow 4–6oz/110–160g per person; 5lb/2.25kg for 20.

Here are some seasonal suggestions.

Autumn into Winter – Hot Vegetables

Ragoût of Peppers and Onions

Allow 3 large peppers and 2 onions and 2 Tbsp oil for every 6 guests.

Stew warm-coloured peppers (not green) cut in strips with sliced onions in olive oil for 40 minutes, taking the lid off for the last 15 minutes to thicken the juices. Season to taste.

Runner Beans

Allow 1½lb/700g for 6–8 guests.

Steam or boil in salted water until just tender. Drain and dress with butter and chopped parsley.

Carrot and Swede Mash

Allow 1½lb/700g for 6–8 guests.

Cut carrots and swedes into even-sized chunks and boil together in a large saucepan till well cooked. Drain and mash together with 4oz/110g butter for every 1½lb/700g vegetables.

Potato and Celeriac Mash

Allow 2lb/900g for 6–8 guests.

Cut even weights of potato and celeriac, peeled, into chunks and boil together in salted water until tender all through. Drain (keep the liquid for soup) and mash with 4oz/110g butter to 2lb/900g vegetables.

Braised Red Cabbage

A 3lb/1.35kg cabbage will feed 20–25.

For these numbers, chop 3 large onions and soften in 3oz/75g butter in a large heavy casserole. Add 1 Tbsp crushed allspice and turn about. Add the cabbage, finely sliced, including core, and stir it around. Now add 3 Tbsp red wine vinegar and 2 tsp sugar, *or* a glass of red wine (dregs from a party will do). Season with salt and pepper, cover and cook very gently for 45 minutes or more. It can sit in a very low oven for 2 or 3 hours.

Optional: add 1–2 peeled and chopped cooking apples after the cabbage.

Reheats well and freezes well.

Gratin Dauphinois

For every 6 guests allow 2lb/900g potatoes, ½ pint/300ml milk and ¼ pint/150ml double cream plus 3oz/75g butter and 1 large clove garlic.

Butter a shallow gratin dish well and dot some crushed garlic over it. Slice the peeled potatoes very thin and plunge into boiling salted water for 3 minutes. Drain and dry. Layer the potatoes into the dish, seasoning each layer with salt and pepper and garlic and dots of butter. Finish by pouring over the cream, then pour in the warm milk, letting it permeate the dish. Dot with butter again and bake in a hottish oven – about 40 minutes at Gas 6/400F/200C – or in a lower oven for longer; it is very amenable.

Braised Vegetables

Use celery, fennel or chicory.

Allow 8oz/225g weight per person – 5lb/2.3kg for 10–12 guests. Whichever vegetable you choose, buy as fat and firm as possible. Cut large chicories in half or even quarters lengthways, and large fennel bulbs in quarters. Celery should be hearty and solid, cut into 4–5in/10–13cm lengths and the heart end into 2 or 4 lengths. Blanch in boiling salted water for 4 minutes, then drain and lay in a shallow baking dish with 2oz/50g butter per 1½lb/700g vegetables and the juice of a small lemon.

Cover with foil and bake for 30 minutes in a moderate oven.

POTATOES À LA BOULANGÈRE

A very useful dish of hot potatoes and onions which will sit in a low oven for hours if need be. Choose large potatoes (fewer to peel), allowing 6–8oz/160–225g per portion, and a large gratin dish or roasting pan.

For 6–8	*For 20*
3lb/1.35kg potatoes, peeled	8lb/3.6kg potatoes, peeled
2 large onions, peeled and chopped	4–5 large onions, peeled and chopped
6fl oz/175ml hot stock	15fl oz/450ml hot stock
6fl oz/175ml milk	15fl oz/450ml milk
3oz/75g butter	7oz/190g butter
salt and pepper	salt and pepper

Preheat the oven to Gas 4/350F/180C.

Butter your dish or dishes thickly, bottom and sides. Slice the potatoes thinly. Arrange a layer of potatoes, scatter some onion over and season with salt and freshly ground pepper. Repeat the layers until all is in, finishing with a layer of potatoes, seasoned. Pour the stock and milk over, dot the rest of the butter over the top and bake in the oven for 45 minutes, until the top is brown and the potatoes underneath are soft.

Note: This is a very flexible recipe. You can use leeks instead of onion, all stock and no milk, and cook it in a higher or lower oven. Chicken stock is good but a well seasoned vegetable stock is fine.

RATATOUILLE

A vegetable dish which can become a meal in its own right: ratatouille, which is such a useful accompaniment to meals for large numbers, being universally liked, reheatable and good cold as a salad. Make more than you think you will need and you won't regret it. No need to salt the aubergines first; modern ones don't seem to have any bitter juices. But do season the dish well.

For 6–8	*For 20*
4 Tbsp olive oil	6 Tbsp olive oil
2 large onions, sliced	5 large onions, sliced
2 large aubergines, sliced or cubed	5–6 large aubergines, sliced or cubed
2 large red or yellow peppers, halved and sliced	5 large red or yellow peppers, halved and sliced
3 large courgettes, sliced or cubed	8 large courgettes, sliced or cubed
1lb/450g ripe tomatoes (*or* a 14oz/400g tin), cut up roughly	2½lb/1.2kg ripe tomatoes (*or* 3 × 14oz/400g tins), cut up roughly
2 cloves garlic, crushed	5 cloves garlic, crushed
1 tsp coriander seeds, crushed	2 tsp coriander seeds, crushed
salt and pepper, sugar, wine vinegar	salt and pepper, sugar, wine vinegar
chopped parsley or basil to serve	chopped parsley or basil to serve

Decide whether you want a chunky stew or a finer one and cut your vegetables accordingly. Heat the oil in a large heavy pan. Add the sliced onion and soften without browning. Add the aubergine and stir that around in the oil, then the peppers, and cover and simmer for 15 minutes over gentle heat.

Then add the courgettes, tomatoes, garlic and coriander and simmer it all together, uncovered, over a medium heat.

Season with salt and pepper and, to help bring out the flavour of the tomatoes, a teaspoon of sugar and a dessertspoon of wine vinegar. Let it all cook uncovered until the vegetables are tender but not mushy and the watery juices have reduced nicely. This will take longer, of course, with the larger quantity.

Serve hot alongside pork or chicken or fish, warm, or cold as a salad.

Autumn into Winter – Salads

Mixed Bean Salad

Green beans cooked al dente, frozen broad beans, cooked, and tinned red kidney beans, in the proportion 4:2:1, dressed with a garlicky vinaigrette and plenty of chopped parsley. For example, 4lb/1.8kg green beans, 2lb/900g broad beans and 1 × 14oz/400g tin kidney beans will feed 20–25 guests.

Waldorf Salad

2 heads celery, chopped, with 1½lb/700g eating apples (cored but peel on), also chopped, and 6–8oz/160–225g walnut pieces, dressed with ½ pint/300ml mayonnaise, serves 10–12.

Aubergines in Yogurt

Allow 2lb/900g aubergines for 8–10 guests, with 4 cloves garlic, ¼ pint/150ml olive oil and 1 pint/800ml yogurt.

Slice the aubergines in ½in/1cm slices and fry in hot oil until browned on each side. Fry the sliced garlic alongside. Salt the yogurt and season with dried mint or crushed cumin and black pepper. Make layers of yogurt and aubergine in a serving dish with garlic and any oil remaining, finishing with yogurt.

Carrot Salad

Allow 1 medium carrot per person.

Grate the carrots as fine or coarse as you like into a bowl and sprinkle with lemon juice to prevent discolouring. Dress with a slightly garlicky lemon and oil dressing (sunflower rather than olive) and serve with plenty of chopped parsley mixed through, from a green or blue dish if possible.

CHICORY, ORANGE AND FENNEL SALAD

Chicory and orange with crunchy fennel make a lovely salad, set off by a creamy orange vinaigrette dressing. For larger numbers, it is more economical to use Chinese leaf as well.

For 6–8	*For 20*
	1 large Chinese leaf
4 heads chicory	4 heads chicory
2 large fennel bulbs	3 large fennel bulbs
2 large oranges	4 large oranges
1 small clove garlic	1 large clove garlic
salt	salt
1 tsp French mustard	1 Tbsp French mustard
3 Tbsp olive oil	5 Tbsp olive oil
1 Tbsp white wine vinegar	2 Tbsp white wine vinegar
¼ pint/150ml single cream	½ pint/300ml single cream

Rinse and wipe dry the Chinese leaf (if used), chicory and fennel. Slice them into bite-size pieces or across into rings and put them in a large bowl.

Grate the peel of 1 orange finely (2 for the larger recipe) onto a plate. You will need it for the dressing.

Cut the flesh from all the oranges: stand each in turn on a board and pare the peel and the pith off with a serrated knife. If they are tender navels, simply slice them across and halve the rounds; if the membrane is tough, slice out each segment with your sharp knife. Either way, keep the juice that escapes. Add the orange pieces to the salad in the bowl.

Now for the dressing: crush the garlic with a little salt in a small bowl and mix in the grated orange peel. Add the mustard, oil and vinegar and stir briskly to make a vinaigrette. Then add the cream and mix in well. Taste and add more salt if you like. No pepper. Dress no more than one hour before serving.

COLESLAW

Coleslaw is not as ubiquitous as it once was but it remains a good choice for a robust winter salad; it is economical and can be made well in advance, even the day before. You can vary the ingredients, of course, though I think that as well as the basic cabbage, a coleslaw should always include a little onion and some sweet apple. Here is a very simple version.

For 6–8	*For 20*
1lb white cabbage	2lb white cabbage
½ small onion	1 small onion
1 large crisp eating apple, skin on	2 large crisp eating apples, skin on
1 stick celery	2 sticks celery
1 large carrot	2 large carrots
½lb/225g jar mayonnaise	1lb/450g jar mayonnaise
oil and wine vinegar	oil and wine vinegar
salt and pepper	salt and pepper
½–1 tsp cumin seed, roughly crushed	½–1 tsp cumin seed, roughly crushed
a handful of sultanas	2 handfuls of sultanas

First, slice the cabbage finely and put it into a large bowl of very cold, salted water. Leave it to crisp up while you prepare the other vegetables (it can be left for an hour or so). Peel and chop the onion; chop the apple without peeling; chop the celery and grate the carrot.

In a bowl large enough to take the salad, mix the mayonnaise with some extra oil and vinegar to extend it (2 Tbsp oil to 1 Tbsp vinegar), season with salt and pepper and stir in the cumin.

Now drain the cabbage well, shaking off excess water, and turn it into the bowl, mixing it thoroughly with the dressing. Add the apple, onion, celery and carrot and turn them all over to coat with the mayonnaise. Stir in a small handful of sultanas. Taste and adjust the seasoning.

Spring into Summer – Hot Vegetables

Early spring can seem more like winter and in England new crop vegetables may be slow to appear. Keep your eyes open in the market for first arrivals and meanwhile use end-of-winter staples like leeks, white cabbage and even dried beans – pale green flageolets have a promise of spring about them.

There should be no problem, once the summer is under way, with finding new season young vegetables. Treat them with respect: whereas winter roots – carrots, turnips, parsnips – need robust dressing with lemon and sugar, the new summer crop should shine with just a little butter and a sprinkle of fresh herbs.

Young Turnips

Glaze them whole by boiling till almost done, then finishing off in butter and a little sugar to caramelise them.

Broad Beans

Young broad beans can be cooked in the pod – much more economical and very good dressed with parsley sauce made with their water.

New Potatoes

New potatoes are a real treat when they begin to come in, especially if you have resisted those year-round imports. Steam them in their skins and turn them in butter with a few chopped chives to serve.

LEEKS IN A SAUCE

Leeks are a wonderful cold season vegetable, coming to their end by the spring. They do shrink with cooking and one way to stretch them is to use the water which comes from them as they cook to make a sauce to cover the leeks. This is also the best way to serve them for a party as they will keep hot for some time.

Allow 6oz/160g per person if served in sauce alongside other vegetables. So for 10–12 people, clean and cut into 1in/2.5cm slices 4lb/1.8kg leeks, weighing after trimming, and boil them in a little slightly salted water until just tender – about 5–8 minutes. Drain them well, preserving the water.

Now melt 2oz/50g butter in a medium-sized pan and stir in 2 Tbsp flour to make a roux. Add about ½ pint/150ml of the hot leek water gradually, then the same amount of milk, then more water to make a smooth pouring sauce, not too thin. Taste and add pepper if you like.

Let it cook gently for a few minutes, then stir in the drained leeks and keep them in the pan in a warm place until ready to serve. Or put them straight into the serving dish and keep in a very low oven.

Note: The leeks may give out a little more water as they sit in the sauce, so stir them around before serving.

GREEN FLAGEOLET BEANS WITH CREAM

! overnight soaking needed

This is a French favourite, often served with lamb but equally good with hot ham. The garlic, parsley, lemon and cream combine to set off the beans beautifully. Double everything for 20.

For 6–8

1lb/450g dried flageolet beans, soaked overnight
2oz/50g butter
a good bunch of parsley, chopped
1–2 cloves garlic, finely chopped
grated rind of 1 small lemon
5fl oz/150ml double cream

Boil the soaked and drained beans in plenty of unsalted water until tender but not collapsed – 20–40 minutes, depending on their age. Drain.

Melt the butter in a large saucepan and stir in the parsley, garlic and lemon rind. After a couple of minutes, add the beans, stir around to mix well, season to taste and stir in the cream.

Serve hot. They will sit happily in a warm place while you carve the ham.

WHITE CABBAGE WITH CUMIN

Cut a hard white cabbage in quarters, cut out the hard core and slice it up, then slice each quarter thinly. Put into cold salted water while you chop an onion or two and soften it in melted butter in a heavy casserole.

Add 1 tsp or more of whole cumin seed and turn with the onion. Then add the cabbage (with the water clinging to it but no more) and turn that in the butter too. Salt and pepper, cover with the lid and cook gently over a low heat until tender – about 30 minutes. Taste and adjust seasoning.

This will hold well for a party and is good with beef or ham or pork.

For 12–15, use 2lb/1kg cabbage, 2 onions, 2oz/50g butter and 2 tsp cumin.

Spring into Summer – Salads

Potato Salad

Choose waxy potatoes, allowing 6–8oz/160–225g per person (the more people, the less per person). Scrub, then boil or steam them in their skins, until *just* cooked through. Drain and peel them while hot (unless very new, which don't need peeling), cut up and dress *while still warm* with plenty of vinaigrette (see Green Salad, page 193) and lots of chopped spring onion and chopped parsley. The onion element is important, so use finely chopped ordinary onion or shallot if not spring onions. The warm potatoes will absorb the dressing nicely.

Rice Salad

Use a risotto rice, easy-cook long grain rice or brown rice so that there is no danger of a mush. Allow 2oz/50g per person. Boil in plenty of salted water until just tender – 10–12 minutes for white, 30 for brown rice. Drain and dress in vinaigrette (see Green Salad, page 193), season with salt and pepper. In summer, add chopped red pepper, diced cucumber and skinned chopped tomatoes with plenty of chopped green herbs. In winter, try chopped dried apricots and a few currants, some crushed coriander seeds and just before serving some toasted almonds or pine nuts.

Pasta Salad

Allow 2oz/50g per person. Choose an open shape – farfalle or shells rather than solid macaroni-style pasta.

Boil until just tender in lots of salted water – 8–10 minutes. Drain, rinse in cold water, then drain again, thoroughly. Dress immediately in a large bowl with vinaigrette (see Green Salad, below) with chopped herbs *or* with a jar of pesto (olive oil, basil, pine nuts, parmesan in a paste), making sure each piece of pasta is coated. Add a little more oil before serving if it looks sticky.

Tomato Salad

Slice ripe, well seasoned tomatoes into a pretty dish, tear up basil leaves to scatter over, season with salt and pepper and drizzle with olive oil just before serving. If you add slices of fresh mozzarella, you have a delicious lunch dish. Allow 1 medium tomato per person.

Green Salad

Choose a variety of green leaves – a crisp cos or Little Gem, some rocket or sorrel or watercress to give a zip, chicory or Chinese leaf in winter. Add other textures if you like – chopped celery or cucumber – then some green herbs: flat leaf parsley, coriander, chives, or whatever you've got to hand. Allow a medium-size lettuce for every 4–5 guests. Dress in a large white bowl with vinaigrette: ½ pint/150ml olive oil to 2–3 Tbsp wine or cider vinegar, a tiny pinch of sugar, salt and pepper to taste and crushed garlic if you like. Shake it all together in a jar and dress the salad just before serving.

MARINATED MINTY MUSHROOMS

A very useful winter/spring salad, as cultivated mushrooms are available all year round. This is best made several hours before the party.

You need firm closed mushrooms, not necessarily button ones. I buy large cheap 1¾lb/750g packs which make enough for 10–12 people. For this amount of mushrooms, you also need:

For the marinade:

8 Tbsp olive oil
juice of 2 large lemons
4 cloves garlic, finely chopped
4 small onions, sliced finely in rings
2 handfuls fresh mint leaves, chopped
1 heaped Tbsp coriander seeds, roughly crushed
salt and pepper

Wipe the mushrooms clean, slice them thinly downwards and arrange in a shallow serving dish. Put all the other ingredients, seasoned with salt and plenty of black pepper, into a small saucepan. Cover and simmer over low heat for 5–8 minutes. Pour the hot mixture over the mushrooms and leave to cool and marinate for at least 2–3 hours.

Note: If so much olive oil seems extravagant, replace half of it with sunflower oil.

TSATSIKI

Allow 1 large cucumber for 6–8 people, with ¾ pint/450ml creamy yogurt, 2 large cloves garlic, and dried or fresh mint.

Dice the cucumber, peeled (or unpeeled if young and not bitter), put it into the colander and sprinkle with coarse sea salt if possible. Leave for an hour for it to 'sweat', then press out as much liquid as possible and dry in a clean cloth.

While the cucumber is sweating, crush the garlic and stir into the yogurt in a large bowl with 1 tsp dried mint or 3 Tbsp fresh mint, chopped. Season with a grind or two of black pepper – no more salt. Half an hour before the meal, stir the dried cucumber into the seasoned yogurt and put it into a pretty serving bowl. Delicious as an accompaniment to spicy dishes or as part of a cold buffet, and very easy to multiply.

BULGHUR WHEAT SALAD

A very good alternative to rice salad because bulghur only needs soaking, not cooking. It also needs robust seasoning, so taste as you go. You can of course vary the ingredients and the seasoning as you like, but chopped green herbs are good on the eyes as well as taste buds. Allow about 1oz/25g bulghur per portion. This salad can be made an hour or two before it is needed.

For 6–8	*For 20*
8oz/225g bulghur wheat	1lb/450g bulghur wheat
8oz/225g dessert apples, cored and sliced but not peeled	1lb/450g dessert apples, cored and sliced but not peeled
1 Tbsp lemon juice	2 Tbsp lemon juice
2 Tbsp wine vinegar	3 Tbsp wine vinegar
4 Tbsp sunflower oil	6 Tbsp sunflower oil
1 clove garlic, crushed	2 cloves garlic, crushed
salt and pepper	salt and pepper
3 Tbsp chopped spring onions	5 Tbsp chopped spring onions
2 Tbsp chopped mint	4 Tbsp chopped mint
2 Tbsp chopped parsley	4 Tbsp chopped parsley
2oz/50g sunflower seeds	3oz/75g sunflower seeds
3oz/75g Fairtrade walnuts, chopped	4oz/110g Fairtrade walnuts, chopped

Put the bulghur in a large bowl and cover with cold water. Leave for 30 minutes, then drain any surplus water. Meanwhile, chop the apples into the lemon juice in a large bowl. Combine the vinegar, oil, garlic and salt and pepper in a screw-top jar and shake well. Add the spring onions, mint and most of the parsley and the drained bulghur to the apples. Stir in the dressing, mixing thoroughly, taste and adjust seasoning. Spread the sunflower seeds on a piece of foil and grill till lightly browned. Stir into the salad with the nuts.

Spoon into a serving dish and scatter with the rest of the parsley.

GREEN PEA SALAD WITH GINGER AND OLIVES ☺

Another creation of Josceline Dimbleby, and a perennial favourite at our summer parties. It goes well with cold salmon, chicken, ham or pork. If there is any over it freezes well.

For 6–8	*For 20*
1lb/450g peas, fresh or frozen	3lb/1.35kg peas, fresh or frozen
3oz/80g pimento-stuffed olives, roughly chopped	9oz/250g pimento-stuffed olives, roughly chopped
3oz/80g candied peel	9oz/250g candied peel
2 small cloves garlic, finely chopped	5 small cloves garlic, finely chopped
1½in/4cm piece of fresh root ginger, peeled and finely chopped	4in/10cm piece of fresh root ginger, peeled and finely chopped
3 Tbsp lemon juice	9 Tbsp lemon juice
4–5 Tbsp sunflower oil	10–12 Tbsp sunflower oil
1½ tsp paprika	4 tsp paprika
a little salt	salt
a large bunch of fresh parsley or mint, finely chopped	plenty of fresh parsley or mint, finely chopped

Put all the ingredients except the fresh herbs into a saucepan. Cover and cook over a medium heat, stirring now and then, for 10 minutes (more for large quantities) until the peas are just cooked.

Remove from the heat and stir in the parsley or mint. When cold, tip into a serving bowl (terracotta looks good) and keep in a cool place. If it has to wait a long time before use, stir it up again before serving, to redistribute the dressing.

Miscellaneous

This final chapter contains those recipes which are not seasonal, and not for main meals. They include a couple of breakfast suggestions, bread for soup, biscuits, teabreads and a chocolate cake for tea parties, party punches and some basic recipes which may be useful.

Truro Porridge
48-hour Dried Fruit Salad
Croûtons
Bread and Bread Rolls
Shortbread Fingers
Cinnamon Biscuits
Fruit Teabread
Banana and Walnut Teabread
Judy's Chocolate Cake
Brown Sugar Meringues
Two Sweet Sauces for Ice Cream
Four Party Pieces
Making Stock: Chicken, Vegetable, Fish and Beef
Blackcurrant Extract and Sauce
Elderflower Cordial
Two Christmas Punches
Kenwood Mayonnaise
Cottage Pie for 60

TRURO PORRIDGE ☺

When I asked fellow bishops' wives for help, this splendid porridge recipe came from Frances Ind in Truro; we have enjoyed it throughout the winter. As she says, it is very healthy and so satisfying, you may not need toast afterwards. The quantities given are for 2 but can easily be multiplied. You can of course experiment with different fruits and substitute honey for maple syrup, but here is the original.

For 2

2oz/50g medium oatmeal
16fl oz water
2 dessertspoons linseed
1 dessertspoon sunflower seeds
2 Fairtrade soft dried apricots, chopped
a few dried cranberries
Greek yogurt or crème fraîche, maple syrup to serve

Place all the ingredients in a pan and stir over medium heat until thickened – 5–10 minutes. Serve with crème fraîche or yogurt and maple syrup alongside for people to help themselves.

Note: Like ordinary porridge, this will keep happily in a very low oven (bottom Aga) if more convenient.

48-HOUR DRIED FRUIT SALAD ☺

! needs to stand for 48 hours

A wonderful addition to the breakfast table, no cooking involved.

For 8–10

1lb/450g Fairtrade dried apricots
4oz/120g Fairtrade raisins
6–8oz/175–225g Fairtrade prunes or dried figs or peaches, or Hunza apricots
4oz/120g Fairtrade almonds, skinned and halved (see note)
2oz/50g pine nuts or unsalted pistachios
4–5oz/120–150g Fairtrade granulated sugar
1 Tbsp each orangeflower water and rose water (from the pharmacy)

Put the fruits, rinsed if necessary, into a large bowl, add the nuts and cover generously with water. Stir in the sugar (to taste) and the scented waters.

Leave in a cool place for 48 hours, stirring occasionally; the juice will be a lovely rich apricot colour and the nuts will gleam white among the dark fruit.

Serve on its own or with good yogurt.

Note: The almonds will taste best if you skin and split them yourself – 2 minutes in boiling water loosens the skin. The flower waters give a genuine Middle Eastern flavour.

CROÛTONS

Cut small squares of bread (white or brown) without crusts from a stale loaf. Fry in a mixture of olive oil and butter until they are golden and crisp all over. Keep warm in a low oven. They freeze well, so you can make them whenever you have stale bread.

Or you can make them in the oven: put the squares of bread in a small deepish ovenproof dish, cover generously with butter and olive oil and put the dish in a hot oven for 20–30 minutes, stirring once or twice. This is a good option if you have an Aga or an oven on for something else. Once crisp, keep them warm in a low oven.

BREAD AND BREAD ROLLS

Homemade soup calls for really good fresh bread to accompany it; shop bread is much better than it used to be but making bread at home is easy and satisfying so here is a basic recipe.

Allow 2½–3½ hours

Makes 2 medium loaves or 24 rolls

2lb/900g stoneground wholemeal or strong white flour – or a mixture
2 tsp salt
½oz/15g fresh yeast or 2 tsp Easyblend dried yeast
1 pint/600ml warm water
2fl oz/60ml vegetable oil

Heat your oven to its minimum temperature or use the lowest Aga oven. Put the flour and salt into a mixing bowl and warm through in the oven for 5–10 minutes.

Make a well in the middle of the flour mixture, crumble the fresh yeast into it and pour in a third of the water, stirring with your fingers. Leave for 5 minutes, then add the rest of the water and the oil. If using Easyblend yeast, simply mix it in with the flour and add the water all at once.

Mix together thoroughly by hand until the dough comes cleanly away from the sides of the bowl. Turn it out onto a floured surface and knead for 5–10 minutes until it is smooth and elastic. Return it to the bowl, cover with clingfilm and leave in a warm place to rise until doubled in size – probably about 1–1½ hours.

For 2 loaves

Turn the dough out again onto a floured surface and knock it back (punch the air out). Divide it into two balls. Oil two medium 2lb/1kg loaf tins and lay a ball in each, shaping into an oblong to fit the tin. Cover again with clingfilm or a damp tea cloth and leave to prove in a warm place, until they rise to within ½in/1cm of the top of the tins – probably about 30–40 minutes.

Meanwhile raise the oven temperature to Gas 8/450F/230C. Bake for 30–40 minutes on a middle shelf. Cool on a rack.

For rolls

After the first rising, take out the dough and knock it back on a floured surface. Then divide the dough into 24 pieces, shape them as you like, put them onto two floured baking sheets to prove for about half an hour and bake in the oven at Gas 7/425F/220C for 15 minutes.

SHORTBREAD FINGERS ☺

Genuine Scottish shortbread uses ground rice as well as flour to give a lovely gritty texture. It is good served with fruit desserts or at tea parties, so it is worth making plenty. You will need a shallow baking tray, 10 × 14in/25 × 35cm.

Makes 30–40 fingers

1lb/450g plain flour
8oz/250g ground rice or semolina
8oz/250g Fairtrade caster sugar
1lb/450g butter

Butter the baking tray and preheat the oven to Gas 3/325F/ 170C.

Put all the dry ingredients into a mixer bowl or processor. Add the butter, cut into small pieces, and either rub in or process till it is like fine breadcrumbs. Tip it into the tin and press into all the corners. Prick all over with a fork and bake in the oven until a pale biscuit colour – about 40 minutes. Try not to overbake.

Leave to cool for about 5 minutes, then cut into fingers and lift out with a palette knife to finish cooling on a wire rack.

CINNAMON BISCUITS

These crispy cinnamon biscuits make a good accompaniment to fruit salads and ice cream as well as being excellent with coffee. This is a Jewish recipe, so uses margarine, not butter, to be dairy-free.

You will need a cutter 2in/5cm in diameter.

Makes about 50 biscuits

8oz/225g self-raising flour
4oz/110g margarine
4oz/110g Fairtrade soft light brown sugar
a pinch of bicarbonate of soda
½ tsp cinnamon
2 tsp orange juice
1 egg, separated
2 Tbsp Fairtrade caster sugar, mixed with ½ tsp cinnamon

Preheat the oven to Gas 5/375F/190C.

Put the flour in a large bowl and rub in the margarine (or use a processor). Add the brown sugar, bicarbonate of soda and cinnamon. Add the orange juice, egg yolk and enough white (not all) to form a dough.

Roll out half the dough thinly on a floured surface and cut into rounds. Repeat with the rest of the dough. Lay the pieces on flat greased baking sheets. Beat the remaining white of egg with a fork and brush each biscuit with the egg white. Sprinkle with the sugar and cinnamon mixture. Bake for 15–20 minutes; the biscuits will crisp as they cool and look very appetising with the sugar glaze.

FRUIT TEABREAD ☺

! overnight soaking (or cooling time) needed

The technique of soaking dried fruit in tea is a traditional British one; it makes for a wonderfully moist, well flavoured loaf, delicious thinly sliced and well buttered. It improves with keeping for a few days, which makes it even more useful. I always make 2 loaves for music weekends, to feed singers and players at the tea break.

For 10–12

8–12oz/225–350g Fairtrade dried mixed fruit and peel
4oz/110g Fairtrade muscovado sugar
8fl oz/225ml cold Fairtrade Indian tea
8oz/225g self-raising flour
1 free-range egg

Stir together the dried fruit and peel, sugar and tea. Leave to soak overnight, *or* bring to the boil, simmer for 20 minutes and leave to cool.

Grease a 2lb/1kg loaf tin and line the base with baking parchment. Preheat the oven to Gas 4/350F/180C.

Beat the flour and egg into the fruit mixture, pour into the tin and bake for 1 hour, then turn the heat down to Gas 3/325F/170C for another half an hour.

Turn out to cool and slice when cold.

BANANA AND WALNUT TEABREAD

Fairtrade bananas are easy to come by in most supermarkets; like all bananas, they sometimes get left to overripen. This is a very good use for those larder lurkers. It is best made in a mixer but you can beat it by hand.

For 10–12

4½oz/125g soft margarine
6oz/175g Fairtrade light brown sugar
2 medium eggs, beaten
grated rind of 1 large orange
12oz/350g self-raising flour
4–5 large Fairtrade bananas, peeled
3oz/75g Fairtrade walnuts, chopped

Grease a 2lb/1kg large loaf tin and line the base with baking parchment. Preheat the oven to Gas 4/350F/180C.

Put the margarine, sugar, eggs, orange rind and flour into the mixer bowl and mix until smooth. Mash the bananas on a deep plate and add them, mix again and then add the chopped walnuts.

Scrape the mixture into the loaf tin and bake in the centre of the oven for 50–60 minutes until well risen, golden and firm to the touch. Leave to cool in the tin for 10 minutes or so, then turn out onto a wire cooling tray.

Serve in slices, as it is or spread with butter.

Note: This loaf keeps well for 2–3 days, wrapped in clingfilm in the fridge.

JUDY'S CHOCOLATE CAKE

Garden tea parties are a feature of our summer life and this scrumptious chocolate cake is much appreciated. Given an electric mixer or processor it is very quick and easy.

You will need an 8in/20cm square tin.

Makes 20 pieces

9oz/250g self-raising flour
1 heaped tsp baking powder
9oz/250g Fairtrade caster sugar
9oz/250g soft margarine
3 large or 4 small free-range eggs
2oz/50g Fairtrade cocoa powder
1 heaped tsp Fairtrade instant coffee
6 Tbsp very hot water

For the icing and filling

7fl oz/200ml tin evaporated milk
8oz/225g Fairtrade granulated sugar
4oz/100g butter
4oz/100g Fairtrade dark chocolate, broken up
1 tsp vanilla essence

Grease your 8in/20cm square tin and line with baking parchment. Preheat the oven to Gas 4/350F/180C.

Sift the flour and the baking powder into the mixer bowl or food processor, add sugar, margarine and eggs. Whiz for a minute to blend. Mix the cocoa and the coffee in the hot water to a paste and add to the mixer bowl. Whiz again until smooth and light. Pour into the prepared tin, smooth the top with a spatula or palette knife and bake in the centre of the oven until firm and springy to the touch – about 45 minutes. Cool in the tin, then turn out.

For the icing/filling, put the sugar and evaporated milk into a small saucepan over low heat. Stir until the sugar has melted, then turn up the heat and bring to the boil. Stop stirring and cook gently for 7 minutes. Pour it into a liquidiser or processor, add the butter, broken chocolate and vanilla and process until thick and creamy (about 30 seconds). Leave till cold.

Slice the cake horizontally, fill with half the icing, then cover the top with the rest.

Guests will need napkins!

BROWN SUGAR MERINGUES

Meringues are so simple to make (and store well in an airtight tin) and are enjoyed by young and old alike. Here is a brown sugar version for a change.

Makes 30–40 medium-sized meringues

4 large free-range egg whites
4oz/110g Fairtrade demerara sugar
4oz/110g Fairtrade granulated sugar

Line 2 or 3 large baking trays with baking parchment. Preheat the oven to Gas ½/225F/110C.

Put the egg whites in a deep bowl and whisk until fairly stiff, then add the sugars gradually, whisking after each addition (an electric whisk helps) until all is in and the mixture is thick and glossy.

Using 2 dessertspoons, spoon the mixture onto the paper making fairly even shaped meringues (don't be too perfectionist). Bake in the oven (lowest part of an Aga) for 2½–3 hours or until they are dried through and crisp to the touch. Cool for 1 hour and store until needed.

To serve, sandwich 2 meringues together with whipped cream or serve as they are alongside fruit salads and ice creams.

TWO SWEET SAUCES FOR ICE CREAM

Chocolate Sauce

This can be made in advance and kept covered in the fridge till needed. Best hot.

Find a cup which holds 7fl oz/200ml for measuring.

Makes approximately ¾ pint/450ml (enough for 8–10)

1 cup Fairtrade granulated sugar
1 cup water
1 tsp vanilla essence
3 level Tbsp Fairtrade cocoa powder
3oz/75g butter
3 Tbsp golden syrup

Put all the ingredients into a saucepan. Bring to the boil and simmer gently for 4–5 minutes, watching that it doesn't boil over.

Toffee Sauce

Makes approximately ½ pint/300ml (enough for 6–8)

4oz/110g butter
6oz/175g Fairtrade light brown sugar
¼ pint/150ml double cream

Heat all the ingredients gently together in a small pan. Stir to dissolve the sugar and melt the butter and bring slowly to the boil. Cook till it has thickened and darkened to a rich caramel colour.

Remove from heat, cool and store in the fridge for up to 2 weeks. Reheat gently when needed.

FOUR PARTY PIECES

Bites and nibbles to go with drinks are a useful part of the party repertoire. Here are four suggestions, three savoury and one sweet, to offer guests.

Cheese Sablés

These crisp cheesy biscuits are delicious to nibble and very simple to make.

Makes 30–40

3oz/75g butter
3oz/75g plain flour
3oz/75g strong hard cheese, grated
salt, pepper and cayenne

Preheat the oven to Gas 6/400F/200C.

Rub the butter into the flour, add the cheese and seasoning and form into a dough. Roll out to ¼in/5mm thick and cut into shapes – stars, circles or whatever. Put onto a baking tray and cook in the oven for 5–10 minutes. Be careful not to overcook them – they are best pale, not golden.

Note: You could brush them with beaten egg and scatter sesame seeds or chopped nuts on top. Or use the mixture for cheese straws.

Savoury and Sweet Tassies

The recipe for these rich little tarts came from a newspaper years ago; we serve the sweet walnut version at Punch and Pie parties, but you can fill the cases with savoury delights as well. You need 4 mini-muffin trays with 12 depressions in each, greased.

Makes 48 small tarts

For the cream cheese pastry

4oz/110g butter
3oz/75g soft cream cheese
5oz/130g plain flour

Cream butter and cheese together and blend in the flour. Divide dough into 4, then each quarter into 12 small balls. Place one ball in each depression; press it with your thumb onto the bottom and up the sides.

For the savoury filling

2 free-range eggs, beaten
3oz/75g strong cheese, finely grated
1 Tbsp single cream
pepper, salt and 1 tsp dry mustard
small pieces of tomato, mushroom, olive, anchovy or ham

Preheat the oven to Gas 5/375F/190C.

Mix the first four ingredients together, seasoning well. Put a small piece of whatever you are using in each uncooked case. Spoon the egg and cheese mixture to fill the cases and bake for 15–20 minutes until risen and golden. Serve warm.

For the sweet filling

1 large free-range egg, beaten
5oz/130g Fairtrade light brown sugar
1 tsp vanilla essence
1oz/25g butter, melted
6oz/160g Fairtrade walnuts, chopped

Preheat the oven to Gas 4/350F/180C. Mix all the ingredients together and fill the cases. Bake for 25 minutes until golden on top.

Each of these recipes fills all 48 spaces. The sweet ones keep in a tin for a few days, so you could make them first and then use the tins again for the savoury ones. You need so little filling that half quantities are not really practicable. But they are very delicious.

Mini Pizzas

These are always popular too: small rounds of puff pastry spread with tomato sauce and topped with tiny pieces of olive or anchovy, capped with a sliver of mozzarella. Bake for 15 minutes in a hot oven. Serve as soon as you and your guests can handle them.

MAKING STOCK

Chicken Stock

Boil up the chicken carcass and fresh giblets, if possible, with onion, carrot, celery, bay leaf, salt and pepper, all well covered with water. Simmer for 1–2 hours, strain, cool and freeze.

Vegetable Stock

Cut 4 carrots, 3 large onions, 3 sticks of celery and 2 leeks in pieces, put in a large pan with 4 pints of water, a bay leaf and parsley stalks, season with salt and pepper and simmer for 1 hour. Strain, cool and freeze.

Fish Stock

Makes about 1¾ pints/1 litre

Put as much fish skin and bones as you can muster – or ask the fishmonger for some – into a large pan with a sliced onion, a carrot cut in three, a bay leaf, some parsley (with stalks), a dozen black peppercorns, 1½ pints/850ml of water and ¼ pint/150ml of dry white wine. Add a little salt, bring to the boil, cover and simmer for 20–30 minutes. Cool, strain and either use or freeze for another day.

If you can spare more wine (party dregs answer well), that will improve the flavour, as will prawn shells.

Beef Stock

Pressure-cooking cuts down the long hours needed to make good beef stock to 40 minutes. This recipe makes a well flavoured stock which you can dilute for soups and stews.

Makes about 2 pints/1.2 litres

2½lb/1.2kg beef marrowbone, sawn across (ask the butcher)
2 pints/1.2 litres cold water
1 small onion
1 carrot, cut in chunks
1 stick celery, halved, with its leaves
1 small bunch parsley stalks
1 bay leaf
5 whole black peppercorns
1 tsp salt

Put the bones in the pressure-cooker with the water. Bring to the boil, then remove any scum with a metal spoon. Add the rest of the ingredients, put the lid on the cooker and bring up to pressure. Plate the 15lb weight on and cook for 40 minutes. Reduce the pressure by allowing to cool slightly, then place under the cold tap to release. Strain into a bowl, cool completely, remove surface fat and store in a fridge or freezer until needed.

BLACKCURRANT EXTRACT AND SAUCE

Small pots of concentrated fruit extract are very useful in the freezer, for making ice cream parfait (see page 89) or enriching stews instead of wine or port. A very good recipe, from Jane Grigson's *Fruit Book* (Michael Joseph 1982), especially if you grow blackcurrants yourself.

For the extract

Put 3lb/1.5kg blackcurrants into a pan with ¾ pint/500ml water. Cover and cook slowly until the fruit is soft. Tie up the fruit in a clean cloth or jelly bag and hang over a basin to drip (I use an upended tall stool). You should end up with about ¾ pint/500ml of strong extract.

Freeze in 5fl oz/150ml plastic tubs and put some in plastic ice trays, so you can use them in puddings or as an essence in stews.

For the sauce

Put the debris left in the cloth or bag into a clean saucepan and cover with water. Simmer for 20 minutes at least. Process or liquidise to a sludge. Pass through a sieve, pressing the juice and pulp through with a metal spoon, into a measuring jug. For 2¼ pints/1.5 litres of pulp, stir in the juice of 2 oranges, sugar to taste and red wine to bring it up to 3½ pints/2 litres sauce.

Freeze in ½ pint/300ml pots.

Note: I have used the sauce instead of extract in the parfait recipe perfectly successfully.

ELDERFLOWER CORDIAL

! needs 24 hours to infuse

This can be found in supermarkets nowadays but is very easy to make and bottle yourself. Apart from serving it with sparkling water or soda as a refreshing summer drink, it has a special affinity with gooseberries. Add a spoonful to gooseberry compôte or Gooseberry Fool (see page 162).

Elders are normally in flower in May, so overlap nicely with gooseberries. Store in half-litre bottles or jam jars. This recipe should make about 7 pints/4 litres of cordial – give some to your friends.

40 fresh heads of elderflower
4¼lb/2kg Fairtrade granulated sugar
4 large lemons, quartered
5½ pints/3 litres boiling water
2½oz/60g citric acid (try the pharmacy if the supermarket fails)

Pick the elderflowers in sunshine. Shake off dead insects but do not wet. Put in a large bowl or non-corrosive pan with the quartered lemons and the sugar and pour the boiling water on top. Stir until the sugar has dissolved. Leave for 24 hours in a cool place to infuse.

Squeeze the lemons' juice into the bowl and filter the liquid through muslin (or a tea cloth) into a deep bowl or pan with a good pouring lip. Stir in the citric acid. Use a funnel to fill clean bottles or jars. Store in the fridge or a cool larder.

TWO CHRISTMAS PUNCHES

Here are two recipes we have served at Punch and Pie parties at Christmas and Epiphany for the past 25 years. They go down well, so we stick with them.

Provost's Punch

For 20–30

6 bottles of robust red wine
½ bottle cheap (but real) port
¼–½ bottle orange curaçao
1 whole orange, pierced all over with a skewer and stuck with 12 cloves
1 lemon and 1 orange, sliced
2 cinnamon sticks
nutmeg to grate
Fairtrade demerara sugar to taste
boiling water

Put all the ingredients except the fruit into a large, deep pan. Don't add much sugar at first; taste and adjust later. Pour in about 2 pints/1.2 litres of boiling water and stir over a low flame until the sugar is dissolved. Now add the orange stuck with cloves and the slices of orange and lemon, pressing out some of the juice as you put them in. Keep hot but never allow to boil. Taste and add more sugar if you like.

To augment the brew during the party, add more red wine and hot water before the first batch is finished; then you won't need more spices or fortified wines.

People are much better about drinking and driving these days, so a non-alcoholic punch is definitely called for and this one seems to answer well.

Camel-drivers' Apple and Ginger Punch

For 10–15

4 litres apple juice
1 litre pineapple juice
1 litre ginger ale
1 large apple stuck with 8 cloves
1 apple and 1 lemon, sliced
2 cinnamon sticks
a 2in/5cm piece of root ginger, bruised
nutmeg to grate
Fairtrade demerara sugar
boiling water

Put all the ingredients into a large deep pan on a low heat, adding the water and sugar to taste. If it seems too sweet, omit the sugar and add more lemon juice. Do not boil.

Note: I have not yet found Fairtrade pineapple juice. Do not substitute tropical fruit juice in this recipe; it will cloud the flavour.

KENWOOD MAYONNAISE

Although handmade mayonnaise, using the best olive oil, is undoubtedly the most delicious, this machine-made version using whole eggs and a mixture of oils is more practical for large numbers and well worth making as an alternative to shop-bought mayonnaise.

To make 1 pint/570ml of mayonnaise, break 2 whole eggs into the liquidiser, add 1 tsp Dijon mustard, 1 Tbsp wine vinegar *or* the juice of ½ lemon, a pinch of salt, and process at high speed for a few seconds.

Then gradually add a pint of olive oil (or sunflower, or a mixture), pouring it in a thin but steady stream through the liquidiser lid onto the egg mixture. Stop when all is added and taste. Add more lemon or salt if need be. Keep, covered, in the fridge for up to a week.

COTTAGE PIE FOR 60

Most of the recipes in this book are for home cooks who find themselves cooking for more mouths than usual. They may be using their largest pans and baking trays but are not reckoning on institutional-size catering equipment. So this recipe is included for interest, though it does work if you do have the equipment. When my friend Joan and I started the Portsmouth Cathedral Tuesday Lunch Club in 1982, she may not have imagined that she would still be making cottage pie for the members 25 years on. Here is her well-tested recipe.

Equipment: 4 large saucepans, 3 catering baking trays.

For 60

15lb/7kg potatoes, peeled
8oz/225g butter
salt and pepper
15lb/7kg minced beef
3lb/1.3kg onions, peeled and chopped
2–3 pints/1.2–1.8 litres water
8 Oxo cubes
1 dessertspoon mixed herbs
2 dessertspoons Lea & Perrins Worcestershire sauce
½ loaf brown breadcrumbs
salt and pepper

Divide the potatoes between 2 large saucepans, boil until tender, drain and mash with the butter. Season with salt and pepper.

While the potatoes are cooking, divide the meat and onions between two large saucepans, add 1–1½ pints/600–900ml of water to each pan and crumble 4 Oxo cubes into each. Stir in the herbs and Worcestershire sauce, bring to the boil and simmer for about 2 hours. Stiffen the gravy in each pan with the breadcrumbs. Taste and season accordingly.

Preheat the oven to Gas 7/425F/220C. Divide the two pans of meat between the 3 catering baking trays and top with the mashed potato.

Bake for 1½–2 hours, turning the oven down to Gas 3/325F/170C when the top is well browned. To serve, divide each tray in 4 longways and in 5 crossways to get 60 portions in all.

Serve with colourful vegetables – carrots and spring greens perhaps.

Select Bibliography

Recommended for further reference and reading for pleasure:

Cox, Nicola (1986) *Good Food from Farthinghoe*, Victor Gollancz.

David, Elizabeth (1960) *French Provincial Cooking*, Michael Joseph.

Dimbleby, Josceline (1984) *The Josceline Dimbleby Collection from the Sainsbury Cookbooks*, J Sainsbury plc.

Grigson, Jane (1983) *Jane Grigson's Fruit Book*, Penguin Books.

Macdonald, Claire (1989) *Celebrations*, Bantam Press.

Macdonald, Claire (1986) *Seasonal Cooking*, Corgi Books.

Richardson, Rosamond (1991) *Complete Vegetarian Cooking*, J Sainsbury plc.

Smith, Delia (1993) *Delia Smith's Summer Collection*, BBC Books.

Index